Oh, You Beautiful Doll

Oh, You Beautiful Doll

The 11½" Doll Book of High Fashion

YVONNE RAWSTRON

Photographs by Shannon Gilmour

A PERIGEE BOOK

Perigee Books
are published by
The Putnam Publishing Group
200 Madison Avenue
New York, New York 10016

Library of Congress Cataloging in Publication Data

Rawstron, Yvonne.
  Oh you beautiful doll.

  1. Barbie dolls. 2. Doll clothes. I. Title.
TT175.R38   745.592′21   82-5263
ISBN 0-399-50660-8   AACR2

First Perigee Printing 1982

BOOK DESIGN BY BERNARD SCHLEIFER

Printed in the United States of America

1 2 3 4 5 6 7 8 9

Acknowledgments

*A*NY WRITER will tell you that the importance of encouragement from friends and family can scarcely be over-emphasized.

I have enjoyed an embarrassment of riches throughout the production of this book, and while it is impossible to mention every single individual whose encouragement warmed me, I must name a few very special people.

First, Marion Stuart, who came up with the original idea for the book and without whose continuing moral support I would never have finished it, my heartfelt appreciation.

Thanks to Anne Lecture for advice freely given from her particular areas of competence, and to Ann Cherekovsky for her generous offer to loan me her miniature silver tea set as a prop for photography.

Belated gratitude to Kate Coleman and Edy Keeler for encouragement and outright nudges when I was tempted to procrastinate.

Special assistance from fellow printers in the composing room of the San Francisco Newspaper Printing Agency where I have worked for ten years: Jack Locke, Joe Virgil and Bill Bird offered technical advice on page layout and makeup for the presentation of my original proposal to the publisher. Hal McDowell, Pat Kimmel, Jane Brooke and Mariano Valderrama gave generously of their time for the actual production of this early work.

Warm appreciation to my agent, Kathy P. Robbins, of Robbins & Covey Associates; to my editor, Sam Mitnick of Putnam's; and to my photographer, Shannon R. Gilmour, for professional assistance above and beyond the call of duty in the form of creative suggestions on ways of making this a better book.

Last of all, to my three children, for listening and responding to my intermittent complaints about the difficulty of working full time as a printer while assembling this book. They all offered moral support at every juncture, and my son volunteered financial assistance when the only sensible action was for me to take time off my job.

Contents

Introduction: Confessions of a Doll Freak   11

ONE: Before You Begin   15

TWO: Casual Wear: First Sewing Projects   23

THREE: Haute Couture   55

FOUR: Lingerie   83

FIVE: The Evening Gowns   103

SIX: Fur and Leather   131

SEVEN: Coats, Jackets, Capes, Stoles, and Shawls   143

EIGHT: The Accessories   161

NINE: Wedding Dresses   169

TEN: Styling Your Doll's Hair   175

ELEVEN: The Props and The Photography   181

Index   189

Oh, You Beautiful Doll

Confessions of a Doll Freak

*M*AKING CLOTHES and dressing a doll can be a lot of fun. The serious Fashion Doll owner already knows it is possible to make clothes for your dolls, because inevitably someone has done it for you, if you haven't done it yourself. You also know you can buy ready-made garments in any department store or toy store that has an extensive Barbie ® Doll display.

What you may not know is that you can become your own favorite designer, you can design and make everything your Fashion Doll wears, from lingerie to ultrahigh fashion evening gowns, brocade coats, and fur wraps. In effect, you can make anything that strikes your fancy. A quick look through any of the slick fashion magazines will kindle the imagination of a potential doll-dress designer.

If you are a truly serious Doll owner/collector, you are readily identifiable in several specific ways. The special care you take with your doll and your single-minded approach to the Barbie ® Doll department of a toy store are early signs. You, no doubt, have tunnel vision. You look neither to the left nor to the right as you hurry to the doll display, and you're willing to sit for hours on the floor, pawing through racks of doll clothes. Your consuming interest is to give your doll the most beautiful wardrobe available.

Just to give you a little background information on my experience as a doll freak, let me tell you that I have been making clothes for Barbie ® since the year she came out, which was 1959. My oldest daughter, Paige, was seven that year, and her favorite Christmas present was her first Barbie ® Doll with a complete wardrobe I made at night, after her bedtime. The first commercial patterns for the 11½-inch fashion doll weren't available yet, so I had to create my own, to figure out the dimensions from shoulder to waist and from waist to knees, as well as the breast/chest measurement and the shoulder width and waist circumference. Mostly it was just trying things and keeping what worked, while tossing out what didn't. I found out early on that blouses with sleeves do not work under jackets, cardigans, or coats. Sleeveless blouses, of course. Later I designed a dickie, which I notice from the fashion magazines are back in style. The dickie pattern is in Chapter Eight.

I taught my daughters to sew for their dolls, in the same way I learned from my Auntie Lois, first sewing everything by hand and then on the machine. They are both excellent seamstresses now and make many of their own clothes.

My father made closets for his granddaughters' Barbie ® Doll clothes when they were about nine and eleven years old, at the height of their Barbie® mania. I gave him the dimensions needed—at least twelve inches high, to accommodate all the evening dresses, and as wide as he could make them, because so many hang-up clothes had been made by that time. We had fashioned makeshift closets from shoe boxes, and they worked all right, but they weren't as sturdy as a wooden closet.

The little wooden closets were about fifteen inches high, with a shelf above the clothes rod for hats, bags, and other accessories. They were made of plywood, with sliding doors on tracks, stained and waxed to a high sheen.

I had a brief respite from making doll clothes for Barbie®, perhaps five or six years, when Paige and Shannon were teenagers, interested only in cramming the maximum number of outfits into their own closets, never mind the doll closets tucked away in a corner with other old toys. They had learned to sew during the years of cranking out new wardrobes for their dolls and made many of their own clothes. Of course, I believe, from personal experience, that sewing doll clothes is a perfect way for kids to begin designing and making their own clothes and accessories.

Jennifer Hughes, to whom this book is dedicated, is a very dear twelve-year-old friend of mine. I began making Barbie® Doll clothes for her when she was about six, taught her to use my sewing machine when she was eight, and at her ninth birthday party, I brought a shoebox stuffed with fur coats, velvet evening coats, gold and silver lamé evening dresses, and assorted pantsuits, including the first one I ever made from a pair of long kid gloves, using the thumbs as sleeves.

Her nine party guests were all girls her age, give or take a few months in either direction. I knew that most little girls had Barbie® Dolls, but I was still astonished when my package was opened. The whole group disappeared into Jenny's bedroom to bring out her collection of dolls. It's hard to say whether the celebration was for Jenny or for Barbie®. The kids had to be dragged to the dining room for cake and ice cream and to finish opening presents.

I realized then that there was a very large market for beautifully made doll clothes. I already knew that eight-year-old kids could be taught to use a sewing machine and that they only required a couple of lessons in how to cut out patterns and assemble the pieces. By that age most kids have enough manual dexterity to handle tiny pieces of fabric, leather, and fur, with the additional advantage of small hands and fingers.

I made a little money selling my small creations at street fairs in San Francisco, where I live, and at flea markets all around the Bay Area, but soon realized I couldn't make a living doing this, because no one will pay what the doll clothes are really worth in terms of materials used and time spent. I figured out finally that I was working for less than five dollars an hour, and since my job as a printer pays almost fifteen dollars an hour, it didn't seem likely that I would become an ex-printer any time soon. It was a lot of fun, but impractical in terms of keeping a roof over my head.

I kept on making the doll clothes and my friends continued to shake their heads and make remarks about Santa's Workshop, compulsive hobbyists, and what the *hell* was I going to do with all this stuff, anyway?

Then my friend Marion Stuart had an inspiration. She and I were jogging on our neighborhood track, when she suddenly grabbed my arm and said, "Come on, Vonnie, let's sit down. I have a terrific idea for the doll clothes!"

You should know something about Marion. She's a walking idea factory. She is just full of wonderful ideas for *everyone else*, so I braced myself for her latest inspiration.

"Why not write a pattern book?" she asked.

I tried not to let my face show that I thought it was just another one of her off-the-wall ideas for someone else, something she'd certainly not give two thoughts to doing herself.

"I'll think about it," I promised, knowing I wouldn't. I told what I thought was an out-and-out lie to preserve the peace.

Well, this book didn't materialize by the grace of the gods! I couldn't *stop* thinking about it, however hard I tried, however much I told myself I probably couldn't string two sentences together for an instruction book. I love teaching. Kids or adults, it doesn't matter whom I teach; if they want to learn something I know, I'm in heaven. And I'm a good teacher; my students learn.

I told Marion that since the book was her idea, she should at least make herself available for some free consultation on how to plan a book, how to figure out the progression of chapters in an orderly sequence, and how to explain on paper all the things I had taught my daughters, my friend Jennifer, and a couple of other interested parties.

"Just write the way you talk," she said. "Consider your book an on-going conversation with someone who wants to know everything you've learned. Think about how you explained all this stuff to your kids and to Jenny."

She said I could use her as a sounding board and that she'd be delighted to read anything I wrote and give me some constructive criticism. I refrained from saying that the last thing in the world I wanted to hear was criticism, constructive or otherwise.

I started writing. I hid the chapters as I got them together. I drew all my patterns on individual sheets of paper and stashed them in a plastic see-through folder. Marion went away on vacation and I worked like a beaver while she was gone, thinking I'd show her all the unorganized chapters when she returned.

She loved them and even said my writing was clear and concise. She thought I should organize the material and start sending it around to publishers, which struck terror in my heart. I recalled stories about bathroom walls papered with rejection notices. I felt sure that no serious publisher would give two minutes' consideration to my frivolous little project. I assured her that I would indeed organize my material into some kind of order, but "let's think about publishers later."

My friend Edy Keeler, who is a dress designer, introduced me to another Marion (Woolf) during this period of organizing the material already written. This Marion turned out to be a bona fide writer, whose novel was coming out soon. Edy, who can't keep her mouth shut even after being sworn to secrecy, told Marion about my project.

The rest is history, if I may be permitted a cliché. Marion told her literary agent, and the next thing I knew, I was signed, sealed, and delivered into the hands of this wonderful agent, who sold my book and brought me a contract to sign away my life in the production of what you hold in your hands at this moment.

And so a hobby I thought was pretty frivolous, though a whole lot of fun, has turned into serious work. My daughter Shannon is the photographer for her frivolous mother, and we both hope *Oh, You Beautiful Doll* will bring pleasure to other mothers and daughters.

The models are all Barbie® Dolls or Christie® Dolls, manufactured by the Mattel Company. Some of them are almost twenty years old, so you may not recognize them. All the patterns in this book, while specifically designed for these dolls, will fit all 11½-inch fashion dolls with figures like the Barbie® Doll or the Brooke Shields doll. You may find that you will have to make slight adjustments to custom fit the clothes you make.

As you progress through this book, you will notice that most of the patterns are variations on a basic theme. For instance all the T-shirts, turtlenecks, and cardigans are made from the same basic pattern, with small changes. The jacket pattern can be adapted to several slightly different designs. The ruffled evening skirts are made from the basic long skirt pattern, but extended an inch or two in width to support the weight of the ruffles.

All the instructions for variations are included in each chapter, and those instructions are spelled out each time, so you will not have to return to a previous chapter if you have forgotten earlier guidelines.

Let's have a big cheer for the Mattel Company now, for their graciously granted permission to use their dolls as models for this book. I could have written the book without models, of course, but wouldn't that have been boring? As it is, I believe this is something more than a simple little do-it-yourself pattern book for amateurs, and I trust the reader will agree.

I have been making doll clothes for longer than many of my readers have been on this planet; my daughters learned basic sewing skills by making their own doll clothes when there were no books like this one.

Creating these designs and simplifying them as much as possible before turning them into the garments you see was a lot of fun. But the best part of all was writing *Oh, You Beautiful Doll* for everyone who wants to have the smartest-dressed doll in town. You're about to begin an adventure.

"Happy sewing, everyone!"

Chapter One

Before You Begin

Designing Your Fantasy

FANTASY and role-playing have long been recognized as important functions of the growing number of girls and women who dress Barbie® Dolls for display and competition. This book is designed for those people. The patterns are simplified for the beginning dress designer (seamstress, couturiere), with variations for most of the garments. I encourage you to use your imagination in the creation of an all-round wardrobe for your doll. Although I have provided my own variations on each theme, you will find it is more fun to design and follow through on your own ideas than to simply copy mine.

You will discover you can use almost anything and everything around the house to create props for enhancing your play-fantasy games with dolls. You can develop new ideas from the props used for the pictures in this book, and I trust you will be inspired by the details of how such props were converted from simple, utilitarian gadgets. A coaster holder becomes a dresser, a small jewelry box serves as a hope chest for your doll's trousseau, and the baby grand piano/music box tickles your imagination into seeing your doll as a chanteuse or a concert pianist. All these conversions will tell you something about improvising props for yourself.

Playing with dolls is important because of the opportunity presented for you to act out your fantasies. Designing a fashionable wardrobe for your doll is only one of the many ways you can release your fantasies into the realm of real life. Each article of clothing you design gives your doll a different identity as an extension of you, and each design may include all the various facets of each role.

Your doll will change from a daytime secretary to an evening disco dancer as quickly as you are able to change her clothes. She can be a busy executive, or a mother, or both. *You* can be a doctor, a lawyer, a schoolteacher, a nurse, or an engineer, all through the medium of the clothes you create for your doll.

I have written this book so that you can start at the beginning and work straight through to make a complete wardrobe for your doll. If your doll already has some of the ready-made, mass-produced, commercial doll clothes available in toy stores, you may choose to make the outfits featured in this book to flesh out and complete her wardrobe. Look through the book and choose what you want to make. You can begin at any chapter. Some of the clothes are more difficult to make than others, and if you are a fledgling designer, I suggest you start with something simple, like a basic skirt and blouse, or a pair of pants and a cardigan. After you have made one of the designs and have seen for yourself how easy it is to make these clothes, you will want to try the other patterns and eventually to design and make your own distinctive variations.

Use your imagination—that is my single, most important rule! Once you have mastered the basic patterns and some of the variations I've given you, you may wish to branch out on your own to envision different kinds of trimming and perhaps even to go so far as to change the line of a pattern to achieve an entirely new design. If you see a dress in a fashion magazine or on another doll and you would like to copy it, look through this book to find the pattern or dress that most closely resembles it and is basically cut in the same way. Think about it for a few minutes before you start cutting. Carefully consider the details you would like to add, whether they might be small strips of lace around collar and sleeves, or pleats added to change the line of a skirt, or whatever small individual touches you want to introduce. Make sure you have all the supplies you need before beginning.

How to Set Up

Before starting you should think carefully about the area where you will be sewing. Whether it is a room unto itself (my dream of perfection would be to have a sewing room with everything built to my small scale), or just a corner in a bedroom or the dining room, your sewing area should be arranged in such a way that everything you need is within easy reach. If you are sewing by hand, I suggest you use an adjustable ironing board set to table height. It works well as a cutting table, if you are careful not to cut into the ironing cover, and if it is large enough to hold all your immediate needs for stitching and cutting, i.e., scissors, needles, thread, pincushion, and not the least important, your iron, ready to press down seams as you stitch them. Unfortunately most ironing boards are not stable enough to be used as a sewing *machine* table, even if you have a very lightweight portable. I have a very old Adler machine, which I bought from my sister when she decided she needed something more modern. I'm told that Adler stopped making domestic sewing machines twenty-five years ago, so this is a real treasure, made of heavy-gauge steel. I also have a very light American machine, manufactured in Taiwan, with the dial-a-stitch wheel and all the modern conveniences of such a machine, but it *is* lightweight, and I prefer my old Adler for straight stitching. I have a very heavy, old oak library table, with big claw feet and a shelf underneath attached to all four legs, just above and inside the claw feet. I stack supplies on that shelf, which I also use as a footrest. I sit in a highchair, which brings me to the right height for comfortable sewing. My grandson Diego thinks it is hilarious to watch his grandmother sitting in his old baby chair sewing away, but I tell him it's functional and that's what counts!

I am devoted to the simplicity of clamp-on desk lamps, which can be attached to sewing tables, desks, and ironing boards. I have three of them. They allow me to light very precisely whatever area I happen to be working in. You are urged to make your working area as efficient and simple as possible so all your energy can be directed to creating your own little masterpieces. Functional creativity might be our motto.

Because sewing and cutting can be a messy process, you should keep a wastebasket close at hand and use it as necessary. I find that I have to use the vacuum cleaner a lot when I am sewing, because my apartment is carpeted. If you have an area with bare floor or linoleum, I recommend that you set up there rather than on carpet; it is usually easier to sweep up loose threads and scraps than to haul the vacuum cleaner out of the closet constantly.

Getting Organized

It is always a good idea to organize your current project in such a way that you complete as many steps as possible before you begin to sew. For instance, if you create a design that requires lining, cut out all the garment pieces and lining pieces at the same time. If you are making several of the same garments, say several blouses or dresses of different fabrics, all cut from the same pattern, cut them all out at the same time, stacking the pieces for each separate garment in individual piles. You can store the pieces for each project in plastic sandwich bags to keep them in order until you are ready to use them, perhaps labeling each bag or storing several small bags in one large one with just one label to cover all of them.

Because I am constantly measuring small pieces of fabric, I bought a couple of yardsticks and tacked them to the edges of my sewing table, and a cheap fabric tape measure that I cut into twelve-inch pieces and pinned along the edge of the ironing board cover.

Production-line Sewing

Making doll clothes (like anything else) for mass production poses some interesting, not to mention frustrating, problems. The first thing to learn is that producing one at a time is silly. Instead, cut out ten or twenty garments, perform one sewing sequence on all of them, stack them up, and go on to the next sequence. As an example, suppose you want to make flounced skirts to give as gifts or to be sold in a church bazaar or at a county fair. If you have done any sewing of doll clothes or even of people clothes, you know this is one of the easiest garments to make. You only need the dimensions of the doll (or person) for whom it is being made—a pattern would be superfluous. The main body of this skirt should be a piece of fabric 5 inches wide by 3½ inches deep, and the flounce should be a strip 10 inches by 1½ inches. Waistbands can be narrow strips of the same fabric, or they can be elasticized—dealer's choice. Since I always make these skirts of cotton, I just tear the strips to the correct width and cut them to proper lengths later. Not all fabric will tear straight, but cotton will.

After you have cut the main skirt pieces into 5-inch lengths, and the flounce strips into 10-inch pieces, separate them by size into two stacks. Gather all the large pieces to 3½ inches (waist measurement), then gather the 10-inch strips to 5 inches. At this point I iron the bottom edges of all the larger pieces, turning them under about ¼-inch. Pin that bottom edge to the gathered edge of the flounce, just about midway into the flounce. I only use one pin for each skirt, but you may choose to secure the two pieces with several pins—whatever makes you feel safe. Then simply topstitch the body of the skirt over the gathers of the flounce. We don't discuss the operation of making gathers here, as it is covered in Chapter Three.

The final operation is that of applying waistbands, one after the other, sewing up the backs, and putting a snap at the waist. I always use waistbands for these little skirts, because I think they look neater than an elastic waist. But that's a matter of preference, and if you prefer elastic, don't let me dissuade you. The best way, I think, of applying elastic is to use a three-inch piece, turn the top edge of the skirt under, tack the elastic to the edge with several stitches, and then just stretch it out to the full five inches as you stitch along. The elastic does the actual gathering at the waist. And, of course, eliminate the initial gathers. If you opt for this waist treatment, you can do it first or last. In fact, I wouldn't make any hard and fast rules about the order of performing the various steps—whatever seems most expedient is the best order.

The Designer's Toolbox

A good dressmaker must have proper tools for her work. There is a great variety in quality, from top-notch down to mediocre. I shouldn't have to urge you to get the best you can afford, since working with inferior tools can produce inferior workmanship. This is a basic list of what you need to get started.

A package of assorted needles (sharps, sizes five to ten)

Sewing machine needles, sizes eleven to fourteen, and ball-point needles if you use knit fabric as well as woven fabric

Glover's needles for sewing leather

Thread, cotton-polyester for most fabric, silk for fine and delicate materials

A thimble

Medium-size, sharp scissors; embroidery scissors

Tape measure or yardstick

Pins, both straight (silk pins) and safety

A pin cushion

Chalk (optional)

A portable steamer

A sleeveboard is very useful for pressing these very small garments

Toothpicks (optional)

Rubber cement

Chalk isn't much use on these tiny pattern pieces, but if you're accustomed to using it, help yourself. When I draw my patterns directly on fabric or leather, I use a ball-point pen and cut just inside the drawn lines.

Your thread should match the color of the fabric you are sewing, except when basting, when you need a strong contrast. Use black or white thread for basting, whichever stands out best.

If your scissors have sharp points, it's a good idea to keep them stored with the points in the hole of a spool of thread when you aren't using them.

You will discover a wealth of useful gadgets to invest in when you are ready to move on to more complicated patterns. For larger pattern pieces you may want to own a pair of pinking shears, which have toothed blades that prevent raveling. I urge the reader many times throughout the chapters of this book to use a crochet hook to pull pant legs and fur and leather sleeves right side out after sewing them together on the wrong side of the material; there is also a gadget called a tape needle made specially for pulling tape, ribbon, yarn, or elastic through a narrow band sewn into garments. I have one, but if I'm in a hurry, I still do it the old-fashioned way—with a safety pin. Finally, you should consider getting a needle threader if you have any problem threading needles.

Eventually you'll learn how many thicknesses of fabric you can efficiently cut at one time and whether or not a pair of electric scissors is a good investment in terms of the amount of use you will get out of them.

You will find that you require a particular kind of storage area. I used plastic shoe boxes for a time, because they're exactly the right size for stacking up evening dresses made for the Barbie® Doll. Then I realized the dresses on the bottom were getting crushed, so I put pegboard on the wall behind my sewing machine, bought some plastic hangers in a toy store, and proceeded to store the finished clothes on hangers hung from eight-inch pegs bought in the hardware store.

I also use the pegs for storing materials, especially rolls of ribbon and braid for trimming doll clothes, strips of fur for edging coat collars and cuffs, lace and bias tape as well as all the other little goodies one acquires in the production of doll clothes.

A Word About Fabrics

The huge variety of fabrics is a source of true delight to the Barbie® Doll designer. The ones called silkies are my favorites because of their delicacy. They should be sewn with silk thread, and you must have sharp scissors because they are slippery. They don't wrinkle easily, but must be absolutely wrinkle-free before you sew them, and, of course, before you cut them. They should always be ironed on the wrong side with a cool iron.

Let's divide the fabrics we will use into categories and then into subcategories. The main categories are *natural* and *man-made* fabrics.

NATURAL FABRICS

* Cotton
* Silk
* Linen
* Wool

Of the natural fabrics, my primary concern is weight; the lighter the better for our purposes of making doll clothes. I have rarely used linen, because I have not found any that wasn't too stiff. The problem of wrinkling is horrendous with linen, too.

MAN-MADE FABRICS

* Rayon
* Nylon
* Acetate
* Polyester
* Acrylic
* Spandex
* Ultrasuede and other fake leathers
* Fake fur

I have used all these man-made fibers, including the fake furs and leathers. Buying used clothes in secondhand stores, I have found lots of old rayon and acetate dresses. For some reason I can't explain, these old fabrics seem to hold up well. Perhaps it is as simple an answer as good care.

Fabric Treatment—Weaves and Knits

The three basic weaves for making fabric are plain, twill, and satin. Any natural or man-made fiber can be used to produce these various weaves. The *plain weave* is the strongest of the three. It is the over-and-under woven potholder you made as a child. There are many variations of the plain weave, such as *basket*, which has two or more yarns laid in at once, and *rib*, which has a raised line or rib either vertically or horizontally. Shantung is a plain-weave fabric of thick and thin yarns that produce a slubbed effect. Shantung was originally made only of silk from Shantung Province in China, hence the name. Other examples of plain-weave fabric are: batiste, broadcloth, chambray, flannel, dress linen, challis, and taffeta.

The *twill weave* is almost as durable as plain weave. It presents a diagonal look because filling threads cross the warp threads in a stairstep pattern. Common examples of twill weave are: denim, gabardine, chino, and ticking.

The *satin weave* is least durable. The filling threads loosely float over several warp threads and produce a smooth, shiny finish. Beauty is the aim of this weave of dramatic and textured effects. Common examples of

satin weave are: brocade, slipper satin, and damask.

There are two basic types of knits; *warp knits* and *weft knits*. *Warp knits* tend to be flat and tight, with a horizontal stretch but little vertical give. *Weft knits* look like hand knitting, with stretch in both directions, but more across width than length.

Finally, there is a category of fabrics known as *non-wovens* because the fibers are chemically matted together instead of being woven or knitted. The most luxurious of these fabrics, ultrasuede, has been used in some of the patterns in this book. Used ultrasuede is infinitely preferable to the new fabric for use in doll clothes, because it softens with age. I prefer natural suede to this artful fake, in the same way I prefer natural-fiber material over man-made fiber, however artfully woven, knitted, or chemically matted.

Sources for Fabric

Most of the materials used for the clothes shown in this book come from dresses and other garments I bought in secondhand stores, thrift shops, and flea markets. The one constant exception was the lamé, which gets a tarnished look over time, but all the other fancy, very-expensive-if-bought-new fabrics are secondhand. You can save a great deal of money on brocade, satin, and velvet if you can find used garments in good condition.

All the fur shown in coats and trims in this book was bought from secondhand sources. I did check out the possibility of buying new fur scraps from a furrier, but the price was prohibitive. In a few isolated cases I have been given relatively new fur by friends who were having coats restyled, but even that fur should be classified as used.

In the same way, the leather I have used to make jackets and pants comes mostly from coats and jackets bought secondhand. Many of the leather garments were made from glove leather, and a couple of jackets were made from very fine smooth leather rescued from a small clutch bag with a broken catch.

Once you get the Barbie ® Doll designer inspiration, you will want to search out new sources of old clothing. Perhaps there is an old trunk full of perfectly preserved clothing from the 1920s and 1930s stashed away in your attic. What a treasure trove that could be for cutting up and using now! Garage sales, yard sales, and moving sales are terrific places to find wonderful old clothes, especially if the person staging the sale has just done a thorough from-attic-down-to-basement cleanup. One of my all-time best buys was a child's red velvet dress, which I bought for a mere ten cents, with a big round stain on the front of the skirt. After cutting away the stain, I used the rest of the velvet for robes and pantsuits for my dolls.

I bought at another garage sale an incredibly ugly jacket that was brand-new, made from ultrasuede. The price was two dollars, and I knew from recently pricing ultrasuede in a yardage store at thirty-five dollars per yard that the fabric alone was worth close to fifty dollars. I would have liked it even better if it had been slightly used, but who counts the teeth in a gift horse's mouth? I snapped it up before someone could tell the seller she might as well give it away for nothing!

The jacket had been made by someone who hadn't the foggiest notion what she was doing; a designer's nightmare. I reckoned the price was so low because the owner couldn't bear the sight of such extravagant folly. I still have a few pieces of that beautiful, smoky blue-gray ultrasuede tucked away in a drawer, but I used most of it for pantsuits for the Barbie® Doll, which were displayed and sold in a little specialty shop that carried my line of doll clothes for a couple of years.

What I'm trying to tell you is that with a little imagination and some solid information about fabrics and their uses, you can use forgotten scraps to your own design advantage. Old cotton socks can be used for shirts and pajamas, old gloves in poor condition should never be thrown out if any of the leather is salvageable, because that soft leather can be used for belts, hats, pants, and even jackets or coats if the thumbs are intact to be used for sleeves. Ribbons can be used for trimming or converted into small flowers. Lace should always be saved for trimming, even in very small amounts. I wouldn't dream of tossing out an old lace-trimmed slip without first re-

moving the lace. A fancy button can turn into a belt buckle. All of these found objects can become elegant beginnings of high fashion, if you use your imagination to incorporate them into your designs.

And let's not forget the old-fashioned patchwork skirts and shirts that were in style only a few years ago. They may not be the height of vogue right now, but they are wonderful fun to make, and when the scale is just right, they look darling on our Barbie® Dolls. I especially like them with a crisp white blouse to relieve all that riotous color.

Color Coordination and Fabric Combinations

We should give some thought to materials and color combinations now. I have mentioned fabrics and colors used for the garments shown in the black-and-white pictures. Some are shown on the cover and many more in the fold-out, where you can see firsthand, but it is important for you to express your own taste in color and fabric. Your designs should reflect your preferences rather than a straightforward duplication of my choices.

Mixing shades of the same basic color in an outfit is more often my choice than using two or more colors together. For instance, in matching a blouse to a pantsuit, my preference would invariably be for a different fabric in a slightly lighter or darker shade of the same color of the suit, or if I am using a sweater in a T-shirt print to accent pants or a skirt, the print would pick up the color of the other garment.

As for fabric, I've said already that I prefer natural materials over synthetics if there is a clear choice. The problem is that there isn't often a clear choice, so when I can't find what I want in silk, cotton, or wool, I am prepared to compromise. The synthetic peau de soie, crepe de chine, and tulle are almost as good as the real thing, and the difference in price is great enough to make it an important consideration if you are buying them new. I believe that the synthetics are less likely to wrinkle, also, which is another important consideration for our miniature clothes.

The small portable steamers available in yardage stores are invaluable for blowing wrinkles away, and an absolute necessity if you work with velvet. I used mine more for the photographing of the models you see in this book than I had in years of sewing. The models were packed in big trunks, with about sixty dressed dolls per trunk, hauled on and off airplanes from San Francisco to Salt Lake City, where my photographer has her studio, and, of course, some wrinkling was inevitable. I blew the wrinkles out as soon as they were unpacked. You can see for yourself that the result justified the effort. The steamer is manufactured by several appliance companies and is sold in large department stores and hardware stores, as well as yardage shops. The cost is somewhere between $10.00 and $20.00; I paid $12.99 for mine.

Back to our discussion of fabrics. Our first consideration in choosing any material for any garment must *always* be weight; our model is small to begin with, so our pattern pieces are tiny. We need the lightest, finest, and thinnest material we can find. Old handkerchiefs are wonderful for blouses. Not long ago, when I was poking through a stack of scarves in a twenty-five-cents-apiece basket in a secondhand store, I came upon a pile of old hankies, some trimmed with lace and embroidery, and when I asked if they were twenty-five cents too, I was told that all hankies were a dime apiece. What a score! I haven't used them yet, but they're safely stored in a Ziploc plastic bag.

Take a close look at the skirts, and you will see what I mean about lightweight fabric. I despaired of ever finding a wool fine enough to hold the tiny pleats in place and fit well at the same time, so I was prepared to make only cotton suits and skirts. But as you will observe, I found several very light 100% wools, and when they were pleated so I could see for myself how well they held up, I even went back and made some more pants (having told myself I'd never need to make any more pants) from the same fabric. It would have been a shame not to take advantage of the opportunity to make the suit jackets do double duty for pantsuits.

You will see in Chapter Three a white blouse worn with a burgundy suede cloth skirt that may interest you, because the blouse fabric has very fine tucks. If you are asking yourself whether I am the sort of compulsive perfectionist who would go to all that work, the answer is NO. I saved that fabric from an old blouse. Somehow I knew I would find a way to use it.

Obviously there is no choice about where to put the darts when using this sort of material; they must be side darts rather than up-and-down ones from the waist to the bosom, which would interfere with the line of the tucks. The ensemble looks exactly like what a proper businesswoman would wear to her job. There are no sleeves and no collar. Armholes and neckline are bound with untucked fabric from the same blouse.

The blue cotton plaid suit illustrated in Chapter Three is made from a dress bought at one of San Francisco's thrift shops, straight off the one-dollar bargain rack. It was a dress in a very large size with a circle skirt, which means I probably got the fabric for less than twenty-five cents a yard.

Plaids, Checks, Patterned and Printed Fabrics

Plaids, checks, and any other kind of patterned fabric should be carefully chosen, with a sharp eye to the scale of the pattern, whatever it is, because if it's too large, it won't work well for your Barbie® Doll. A friend of mine who makes stuffed toys and some doll clothes told me she creates her own plaids by adding extra lines of different colored threads when she has a plaid that is almost, but not quite, small enough for her doll clothes. I haven't tried it yet because of my good luck in finding some very tiny ones.

In Chapter Three you will see a gray plaid suit trimmed with white kid-glove leather, which is just a little off-scale, but I had already made it when my friend offered her suggestion.

There are several examples of street dresses made with the basic pattern for the top attached to a pleated skirt (Chapter Three). Most of them are good examples of very tiny prints and plaids.

Chapter Two

Casual Wear: First Sewing Projects

THE PATTERNS IN this book may be used for hand or machine sewing. The major difference between the results is that a sewing machine is faster, easier, and the final results hold up better. On the other hand, because you are working on a small scale, hand stitching will be necessary to finish some of the garments you make.

If you use a machine, be sure that you use the right length of stitch for each article of clothing you make. Small stitches are needed for fine work, and large stitches are needed to pull up gathering. Most of the new domestic (as opposed to industrial) sewing machines have the ability to make a straight stitch, zigzag, and some sort of buttonhole. Some have attachments (or in more expensive models, built-in features) that allow tucking, hemming, and ruffling. These may be of use when you try more advanced patterns, but for the moment, we'll stick to the basics.

Basting

Basting is a series of very long stitches that are used to hold two or more pieces of material together. They are not permanent and should be made with a fine thread that will not leave holes in the fabric.

If you're using a sewing machine, use the longest stitch. This will hold fabric together and is much faster and stronger than hand basting. Always test the machine, basting on a scrap of the fashion fabric to be sure it won't leave needle marks after the thread has been removed.

Seams

You probably already know that a seam is the point at which two pieces of fabric are sewn together. If you are wearing a dress or skirt, lift the hem so that you are looking at the wrong side of the material. Can you see where one piece is joined to another? That seam is made by placing the right sides of the two pieces of fabric together and stitching along the edge on the wrong side.

The simplest way of telling which side of any material is the right one is to lay back a corner of it so you can compare the sides. In general the right one is the one that looks best. You can almost always determine this with your naked eye, and if you can't, it probably doesn't make any difference which side you sew on.

When making seams it's also important that you stitch in the direction of the grain of the fabric. This is especially important if you have an angled or curved area. You can tell which direction the grain runs by running your finger along the cut edge. If the threads seem to spread apart, you're going against the grain. If they stay together and lie smoothly, you're going with the grain. An easy rule to follow is to sew from the widest area of the garment toward the narrowest part. Curved areas (such as the armholes) may require stitching in two directions because the grain may change directions along the curve.

Hems

Having lifted your hem, you can see that it is the turned-up edge of your skirt. Blouses and pants also have hems. There are several ways to hem a garment. The basic one is by hand: working on the wrong side, you turn the edge of the material over twice, once close to the edge, and then again the width you want the hem. Baste it or pin it (using straight pins), or press it in place. Now sew the hem on the wrong side. Slant the needle and take a small stitch (one or two threads) in the garment, close to the hem, and bring the needle up through the hem edge. Be careful not to pull the threads too tight, otherwise the stitches will show. Because the garments you will be making are fairly tiny, there is really no point in discussing at length wide versus narrow hems. As you advance, the variation in width will become a designer touch you can finally decide for yourself.

There is another method of making hems that is easier and faster and will serve almost all the basic clothes to be made from this book. You can use iron-on fusion tape, which you can buy in a yardage shop or the notions department of a five-and-dime store. You may even find this item at the sewing needs display in a large grocery store or supermarket. There are a few tricks to using fusion tape on doll clothes, but we will get to specific instructions for that later in this chapter.

You can, of course, hem all your doll clothes on a sewing machine, but if you don't know how to use the blind-stitch method, or your sewing machine won't do it, a machine

hem can be the least attractive way to finish a garment. I prefer to use fusion tape because there will be no stitches to show on the finished garment.

Darts

The fourth sewing step you must master for these patterns is the dart. Obviously this isn't something you throw at a target! I suspect, however, that the person who came up with the name knew those little spears, because a dart does bear a resemblance to them.

Darts serve the purpose of shaping a garment to the body that will wear it. They tighten material at one point and add fullness at the opposite end of that narrowed point. You will use darts at the waist of the pants pattern that is included in this chapter. They pinch in the waist and add fullness at the hipline. The Barbie ® Doll has a very tiny waist and proportionately large hips, so any garment that is fitted at both waist and hips requires a dart. The other use of the dart in these patterns is to shape bodices to fit tightly over the breast of the Barbie ® Doll. You will see samples in the various evening gowns (see Chapter Four). Remember that when you fit a pattern to the bust line, darts should release fabric at the fullest part of the figure. If bust darts are too low or too high, the fabric will not be released where necessary. Once you have marked (see below) where the dart should be, fold the material, right sides together, and stitch along the marked line of the V-shaped dart.

Marking

In order to put a garment together, darts, construction lines, and placement lines must be transferred from the pattern to the wrong side of the fabric. This step, known as marking, is done while the pattern is still on the fabric. I suggest you back the traced pattern with something substantial, like construction paper or a brown paper bag, before cutting the patterns. I have been doing this for years, especially because I like to draw my patterns directly on the material I'm using.

This is especially important if you want to use a heavy material or leather, and you need something with more substance than tissue paper to draw around. I have found it particularly helpful to use different colors of construction paper for different kinds of patterns. I use pink to back dress patterns, purple for evening gowns, blue for pants, and orange for shirts and blouses. My color choices are arbitrary, but I at least know what color to look for when I'm shuffling through a big stack of patterns.

Cutting Fabric

Before you cut any of the material you're going to use, it's important to make sure the fabric is not wrinkled. Press it before you cut your pattern. Wool material should be pressed with a damp cloth over it, otherwise it gets shiny. Rayon or silk should be pressed on the wrong side with a cool iron.

When you cut the fabric, be sure the edge of the cloth has been cut evenly. If the material has a printed pattern, you can sometimes use the pattern itself as a guide. Some materials tear straight. But when you are working on cloth with neither of these advantages, pull a thread close to the ragged edge—make sure it's a thread that goes across the material—and cut along the line.

Use a pencil or chalk to draw the outlines of your pattern, and cut after you've traced all the lines. If there is any question about how large to cut the garment, pin the seams of the outline before you cut, and try the pattern on the doll. It is always better to cut things too large and then cut them smaller when you find you've made a mistake. Otherwise you waste material by cutting the pattern too small and having to throw it away.

Let's get on with the instructions for our very first pattern, which includes a very basic, sleeveless shirt-sweater to be worn under jackets and cardigans, a vest to be worn over long-sleeved shirts or sweaters, and the cardigan, which converts to a turtleneck sweater by adding a small rolled piece of the same fabric at the neck and wearing the sweater backwards. I hope that doesn't sound complicated, because it is really very simple. The last pattern in this series is for several kinds of pants. The basic straight pants are first, from which are adapted harem pants, knickers or buccaneer pants, pedal pushers, and shorts.

THE SHIRT-SWEATER

You may like another name for the shirt-sweater; it certainly is a very mundane name. I call it that because it serves both purposes, depending on the material used. T-shirt fabric works well, but I really prefer a heavier, looser knit for texture. You will see several varieties of this garment on the models. It can have a modified turtleneck if you cut the material a bit higher in front so that it rolls under, to be secured with a few tiny stitches. If my knit fabric ravels easily, I always use the zigzag stitch around the edges before putting the two pattern pieces together.

You can see that there are no darts on this little garment. I designed it to be made from a stretchy fabric like T-shirt cotton, tightly knit wool or rayon, or even an old machine-knit sweater ready to be thrown away, any or all of which will stretch nicely over your doll's bosom and need no darts for shaping.

The larger pattern piece for this garment is shaped like a very wide U, cut either straight across the top, or rounded if you want a rolled collar to simulate a turtleneck.

The other smaller piece is just a long skinny strip that doesn't look very important. Don't be deceived! This piece forms the waist and shapes the armholes for the little sleeveless shirt.

This pattern was designed specifically to be worn under jackets and coats when I got impatient and tired of using scarves to fill in necklines. By now you are certainly aware that we can't simply pile on layers of clothing: long-sleeved shirts, blouses, and sweaters just do not work under a jacket if the jacket fits well. And, of course, our doll, just like a real live person, looks best in well-fitted clothing.

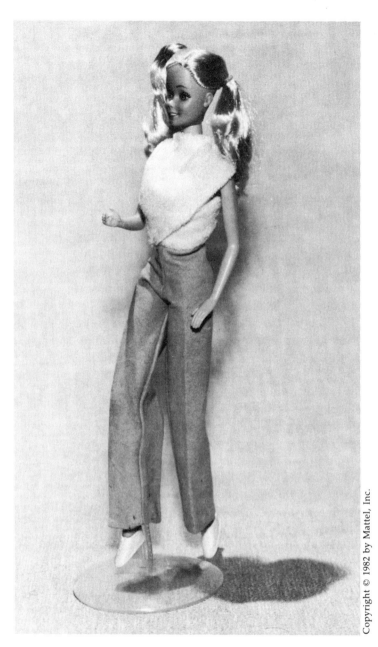

First, hem both pieces, turning the edge under all the way around, unless your fabric doesn't ravel. Then fold the long straight piece to find the exact middle. Place the midpoint of the larger piece on the exact center of the waistband and stitch them together. Now pin the A ends together and stitch the waistband from the center to the A end. Repeat the same operation from the center to the B ends. Put it on your doll, sliding her arms through the obvious armholes, pulling the entire garment together in the back to determine exactly where the snap must be attached.

Wasn't that easy?

A small cautionary note here: If your shirt-sweater seems loose because you are using a very loose-knit fabric, you can simply cut the pattern smaller. It is very hard to be precise for all fabrics when you are using stretchy knits.

The Main Point

Let's not forget that the objective of this book is to make you the designer of your own doll clothes. When I started working on standardizing the patterns herein, I did a lot of fooling around with ideas and testing of possibilities.

The shirt-sweater pattern is the result of my frustration in getting together something really simple to wear under jackets and coats. I am delighted with the end result, but please don't imagine that it worked right the first time. It was too big or too small, too wide or too narrow. In the midst of creating it, I also found that it sometimes works just as well upside down as right side up!

You may have to vary the pattern a little bit, depending on how stretchy your fabric is; everything depends on the amount of stretch and give, and which way the fabric stretches, as well. If you take a close look at all the T-shirts that have cuffs and waistbands, you may be able to see that I used the maximum-stretch direction for cuffs and waistbands.

This doll is called "Your First Barbie®," and this is the hairdo she arrives with. She appears many times as a model but with different hairdos throughout these fashion illustrations, because this little-girl ponytail look is not appropriate for most of the clothes she is modeling.

Here she wears one of the many shirt-sweaters you will be looking at. It is made from a soft, creamy white, nubbly polyester fabric.

The pants are glove suede in an understated lavender shade. She has been turned on the stand so that the inner leg seam can be fully visible, and so you can see the fit at the waist.

Her tennis shoes were bought especially for the sporty pictures shown in this chapter.

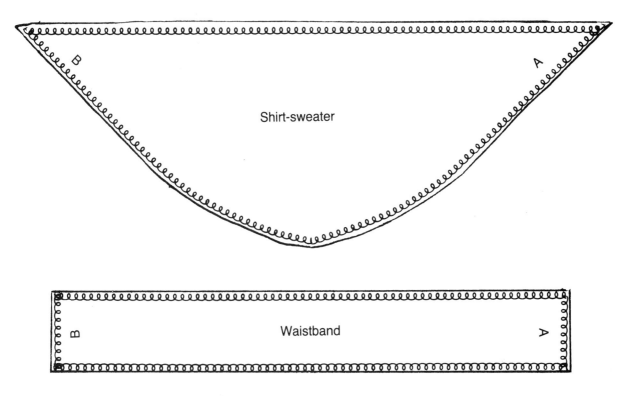

Shirt-sweater

Waistband

ℓℓℓℓℓℓℓℓℓℓℓℓℓℓℓℓℓℓℓℓℓℓ Zigzag or Whipstitch

PATTERN I

Fabric Coordination

Before I start sewing, I always try to organize my supplies. With these first patterns, it is especially important to have a clear idea of what goes with what, both in terms of material and in terms of color. I like to mix textured stretchy fabric in a top with smooth tightly woven material for the pants, although I've had terrific results using very fine, rather loosely woven wool for pants, too.

Color coordination is first of all a matter of taste and preference. I like very much to mix shades of the same basic color, as in the suits in Chapter Three, piping the edges of the jacket with solid color suede cloth and using the same cloth for a matching hat (Chapter Eight). The little sleeveless blouse (Chapter Three) or dickey (Chapter Eight) carries that color scheme one step further.

However, in this chapter we are dealing with sporty clothes, where we have more leeway with contrasting colors. Blue jeans can be worn with any color shirt or sweater, of course, even with stripes, or checks, or flower-print material. On the other hand, if you make pants that are not a solid color, your best bet is to stick to solid-color tops. I think a red sweater is an absolute must for any complete Barbie® Doll wardrobe, but that's just my prejudice. I adore red and wear it a lot, so of course, I will use *any* excuse for making something of red fabric.

As I said earlier, use old clothes or scraps for your first attempts at making doll clothes, especially if you are just beginning to sew. Once you have completed a garment and can see for yourself that some materials work better than others, then use the best fabric you can lay your hands on.

These free-standing dolls may deceive you with their relaxed poses. They are carefully balanced against each other, with the aid of florist clay smeared on the soles of their shoes.

The Golden Dreams Christie® Doll is wearing a new hairdo; her hair is pulled tightly into a ponytail on top of her head, then fanned out around her face, and held in place with hairpins.

Her buccaneer pants are made from ultrasuede, tightly gathered to meet her boots, which have been painted with burgundy nail polish to fit the overall color scheme. Her blouse is made from a polyester tricot requiring no darts to fit nicely over her bosom. The bow tie was constructed separately and attached with a couple of stitches to the blouse.

Her modeling partner, the Golden Dreams Barbie® Doll, wears the hairdo she arrived from the store with. Her pants are made from a soft polyester suede cloth, which is used again in the trim around the long velour overblouse.

Do you recognize this pair? The blond model is Your First Barbie® Doll with a new hairdo. The black model is the Golden Dreams Christie® Doll just as she arrived from the store, hair brushed for smoothness only. They are sitting on a wooden jewelry box, which you will see repeatedly used as a prop, either for sitting on or for leaning against when stood on end.

The blond model shows off a deep, dark purple velvet blazer to complement her cotton buccaneer pants.

The beautiful Christie® Doll wears a royal blue leather blazer over her soft powder-blue shirt-sweater. Her pants are made from very lightweight cotton denim.

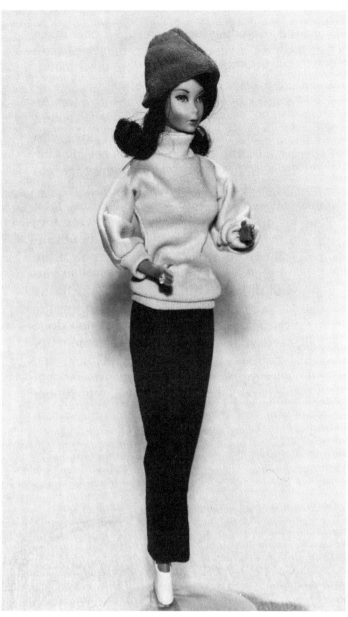

This stunning Barbie® Doll was manufactured at least ten years ago, probably in 1969 or 1970. She has rooted eyelashes and the most marvelous almost-real hair. Quite possibly she is the prettiest doll ever put out by Mattel. Her head has obviously been put on a later-model body.

Her peachy-colored turtleneck sweater is made from medium-weight T-shirt cotton, and the pants are black glove leather. Her little hat is of very soft plushy velour in a hot pinkish-orange color. Sounds like a terrible color combination, doesn't it?

Note the ring on her finger and her tennis shoes.

The Golden Dreams Barbie® Doll wearing a somewhat contrived disco-dancing outfit with buccaneer pants. They started out as harem pants with a crisscross halter top, but the pants weren't really full enough to qualify as harem pants, so I cut them off just below the knee and added the cutoff portion of each leg to the halter as sleeves. The finished product certainly demonstrates the wisdom of improvising as you go along, doesn't it?

Her fancy coiffure and basket-weave, single-strap, wedge-heel slides complete the picture for an evening of dancing.

THE VEST

As you can see, the vest is just one piece, cut on a fold and sewn together on each side at the edges marked "C." The seams are sewn with the right sides together, stitched on the wrong side of the fabric. The dotted lines on the patterns always indicate a seam, and the squiggly lines always indicate a hem, whether it is actually hemmed with needle and thread, or fused, or, in the case of leather, glued.

A vest is very simple to make, especially if you use leather or felt, which will not ravel and doesn't even require a hem in most cases. Although all vests are cut from the same pattern, a smooth leather vest is glued down around the edge to provide a finished look. A suede one is not, because it doesn't need to be and because I like to emphasize the contrast of textures. You can make the decision for yourself based on the kind of material you use.

You can also decide whether or not to make pockets or to add decorative trim around the edges of the vest. When I make pockets for a vest, I just glue them on, carefully positioning them to be sure they line up and are exactly the same size.

To glue down the edges of the vest (or any other leather garment), apply rubber cement with a toothpick, and then roll the edge with the same toothpick, which saves getting glue all over your fingers as you press the edge into place. I have tried several kinds of glue, and they all work if you apply pressure long enough to get a good bond, but a very tiny amount of rubber cement works without running all over the place. You can control the flow of glue better with a toothpick than you can with the wide brush that comes with the bottle. Keep in mind the fact that using the smallest amount of glue to get the job done will save your material from stiffening up, which happens with too much glue. Just wipe off the toothpick with some tissue or a piece of toilet paper when it gets tacky from the rubber cement.

PATTERN II

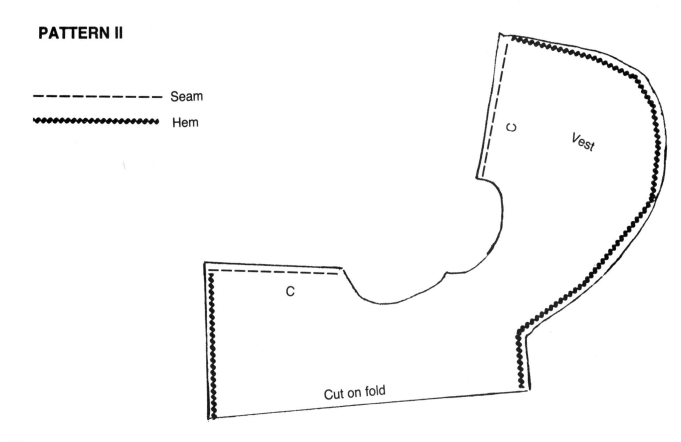

------------- Seam

▰▰▰▰▰▰▰▰▰▰▰ Hem

EXPLANATION TO THE PULL-OUT COLOR POSTER

Beginning at the top, from left to right:

Top Row: Parisian Barbie® wears a pink cotton print evening gown and a mink coat. Hispanic Barbie® models a fake fur evening coat with rabbit fur collar and cuffs.

Middle Row: An old unidentified Barbie® wears a plaid cotton dress, trimmed at the neck and sleeves with stiff white bias tape. Black Barbie® poses in a caramel-colored suede pantsuit. Oriental Barbie® wears a chocolate suede blouse and dark brown wool pants.

Bottom Row: Golden Dreams Barbie® wears a brown wool tunic dress over a matching skirt, highlighted by a leather belt and hat, trimmed with pipe cleaners. The brooch on her collar is actually a pierced earring. Scottish Barbie® wears a pure silk print dress with red bias tape collar, cuffs and waistband.

Beginning at the top, from left to right:

Top Row: Oriental Barbie® wears a gold lamé dress with a gold lurex top, over which she wears a brocade coat for elegant contrast. Hispanic Barbie® poses in this ruffled dress made from a stiff border print. There are only four deep ruffles because the material is difficult to work with. Italian Barbie® is seen in this black taffeta strapless consisting of a tricot half-slip with a lace insert. The bodice is made from sequins.

Middle Row: Black Barbie® wears a phenomenal brocade and lamé pantsuit just made for an eye-catching entrance to a party. Hispanic Barbie® is ready to step out in this red bouclé sweater and plaid skirt.

Bottom Row: Happy Birthday Barbie® displays a suede cloth jogging suit made for a full day out on roller skates. Golden Dreams Christie®, with her hair straight back, wears a beautiful mural print dress made of fine, delicate silk, finished at the neck and sleeves. Parisian Barbie® models this pale green pant-suit made from soft glove leather. The collar and cuffs in suede are merely the reverse side of the leather itself.

Beginning at the top, clockwise:

Black Barbie® models a silver lamé flamenco dress with brocade ruffles. Another Black Barbie® models a red velvet pantsuit with mandarin collar. Ballet Barbie® wears a silver lurex pantsuit with matching headband. A very old Barbie®, possibly twenty years old, with original bubble hairdo, models a cocktail suit which would have been just as fashionable twenty years ago. Scottish Barbie® wears a pantsuit made from a pair of stretchy gloves of a very shiny material. Italian Barbie® wears a white kid glove-leather shirt under her lush mink coat.

Beginning at top, from left to right:

Top Row: Parisian Barbie® in an original wedding dress; Hispanic Barbie® in a "Lady Di" wedding dress; Blonde Barbie® with wedding dress and veil with seed pearls.

Middle Row: Black Barbie® in blue leather jacket with blue shirt and blue pants; Hispanic Barbie® in white and pink border print dress.

Bottom Row: Scottish Barbie® in teal blue tunic dress; Black Barbie® in a red velvet top with lace edging and white leather pants.

This Black Barbie ® Doll appears to be resting after an afternoon of gardening. Note the shears in her left hand and the watering can on the floor, both obviously used for the rose arrangement on the small side table.

She is wearing an outfit of lightweight suede cloth: rust-colored buccaneer pants and a dark blue turtleneck sweater of the same fabric. Her shiny black boots were hand painted with enamel paint.

You may recognize her chair as one of a set put out by Mattel in a ready-to-assemble kit. I covered the back and seat with pale beige suede because the hot pink color on the original chair clashed with some of the models' ensembles. It was just too obtrusive a color even if it hadn't clashed; props should not draw the eye of the observer away from the model.

This blond cutie, who is packaged with two wigs when you buy her, seems pleased with her flower arrangement as she sits for a momentary rest.

Her red buckle shoes match the red cardigan, which is topped with a tiny chiffon scarf. The blue jeans are made from medium-weight denim.

I like her silky natural-looking hairdo, so I just gave it a quick brushup before posing her.

PATTERN III

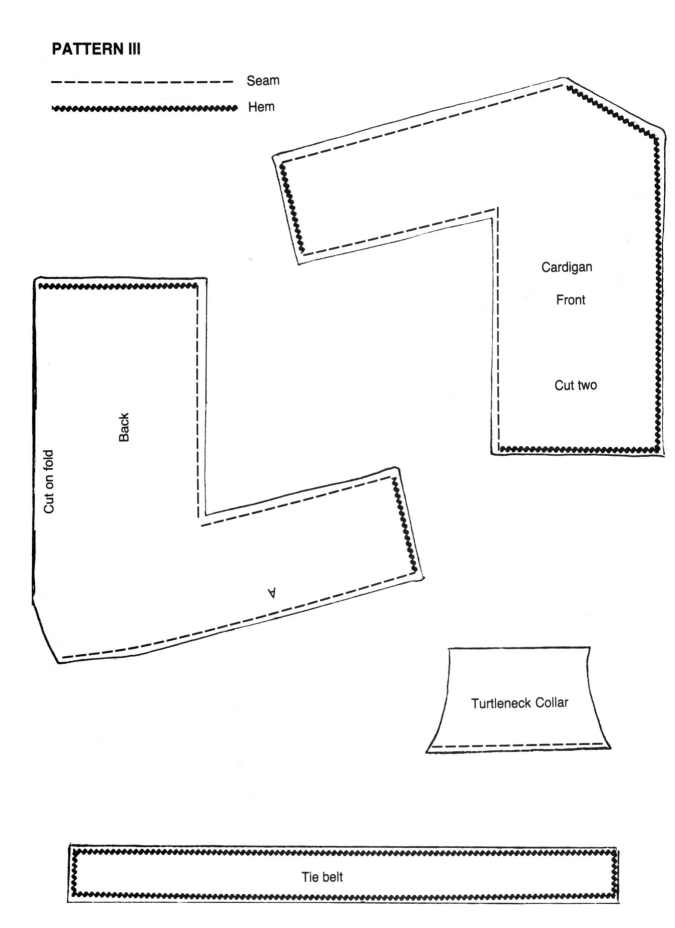

Seam

Hem

Cardigan

Front

Cut two

Back

Cut on fold

A

Turtleneck Collar

Tie belt

THE CARDIGAN

The four pieces of the pattern for the cardigan are the back, which looks like a laid-out sweater, a right front, a left front, and the belt. The back must be cut on a fold (i.e., a piece of fabric folded in half). The two front pieces can be cut at the same time using a doubled or folded piece of fabric; that way, when the second piece is flipped over, both pieces will have the *right* side facing up.

If you are sewing by machine, use the zigzag stitch to finish the edges of the belt by simply folding it down the middle and sewing it together. In this case you sew on the *right* side. If you are sewing by hand, I suggest you use a whipstitch.

Pin the three main pieces together, matching the right front piece to the corresponding side of the back piece and then the left front piece to the other side. Remember, you will be sewing all the pieces together on the *wrong* side. Then sew from the neck edge to the end of the sleeve. Hem the sleeves before continuing on to the next step. Never use glue on knitted fabric.

After the sleeves are hemmed, lay the pieces together again and stitch each under-arm edge from the bottom of the sweater to the sleeve edge. Turn it right-side out, using a crochet hook to pull the sleeves through.

Starting at the bottom edge on either side, hem all around the sweater now, turning under only enough fabric to achieve a neat finished edge. A toothpick can be useful in turning this edge, just sort of rolling it as you go. Toothpicks or wooden skewers are absolutely indispensable for putting these tiny pattern pieces together.

Now try it on your doll. How does it fit?

You haven't forgotten the belt, have you? I fold it in half to find the exact middle before attaching it to the center back of the cardigan. If it's too long, trim off the ends or tie a knot in each end. Stretchy knit material is unpredictable, and I have often ended up with belts that were too long—never too short.

Are you satisfied with the fit and with your workmanship? Would you like it better with pockets?

Go ahead and try it another way if you have leftover material. Cut out a couple of pockets, pin them on from the inside, and check for flaws before actually sewing them on.

You might want to tie a small scarf loosely around your doll's neck at this stage also, to get a different look. Try everything!

THE TURTLENECK

The adaptation from cardigan to turtleneck is quick and easy, since you already know how to make the cardigan. You just attach the small piece marked "turtleneck" to the center back, which will become the front, rolling the top edge of that piece under and securing it with a few stitches. I don't use a belt on my turtleneck sweaters, but I do attach a couple of snaps to hold it together in the back.

An important point to remember when making shirts, blouses, dresses, and sweaters for your doll is that they must be open, either in the back or in the front so that they will go on our dolls with a minimum of fuss and strain. Pulling clothes over the doll's head messes up her hair. Another important consideration is the arms. If she has straight arms, they can be pushed straight back behind her, and both arms slide into the garment at once. Knit fabric will catch on her fingers unless you tape a small piece of fabric over her hands first. Bent arms, which many models of the Barbie® Doll have, present problems if the fabric is not flexible, but I just push the arms back in the same way I do straight arms and carefully slip the sleeves on, pushing them a little bit at a time, until I can pull the arms back into position and straighten the garment, whatever it is, whether a jacket, a coat, or a sweater. This is no problem if the garment is open in the front. If the opening is in the back, you will simply reverse the process, sliding the arms into the sleeves from the front.

The Oriental Barbie® Doll, sitting in the rocking chair, wears a pink Lurex jacket with a silver thread running throughout the fabric, beige leather pants, and pink slides.

Standing behind her, balanced by the chair back, are two First Barbie® Dolls with different hairstyles, a good example of what is possible in varied coiffures. The doll on the left wears a powder-blue turtleneck sweater, made from very lightweight T-shirt material, over brown wool cuffed pants. The wool is a bit heavy for these small dolls, but the line is good, don't you think? Her shiny blue slides lend a perfect final touch.

The doll on the right, with her fancy upsweep, wears a red, white, and blue checkerboard shirt made from Spandex fabric, with a tiny rolled collar, cuffs, and waistband from matching red material. Her white pants and shoes aren't fully visible, but since her shirt is the main attraction, who cares?

This is the Ballet Barbie® Doll with her elaborate hairdo combed out for a sweet natural look.

She models a cardigan that had to be cut very carefully in order to match up the flower patterns on the fabric for the two front pieces. This pattern is repeated across the back of the sweater. Her pants, topstitched down the front of each leg, are made from cerise glove suede, and her pink shoes complement the pink flowers on the sweater as well as the tone of the pants. Isn't she a lovely model?

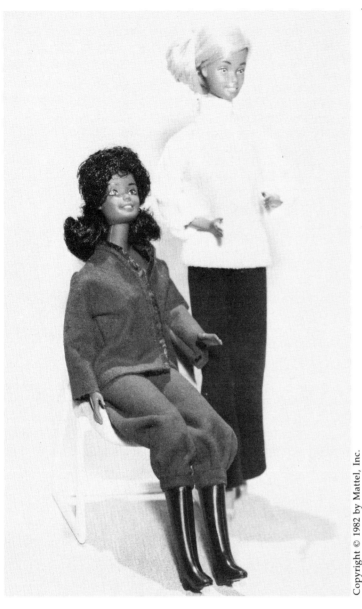

The Beauty Secrets Christie ® Doll wears a rust-colored pantsuit piped with a scarf print that picks up the rusty shade. Her shiny black boots are perfect for this buccaneer pantsuit. She arrives from the store with very long hair, which I have twisted up in back and anchored with a couple of hairpins to give the illusion of shoulder-length hair.

The Malibu Barbie ® Doll, on the right, wears a white turtleneck shirt made from an old one I was ready to toss out. The sleeves are cuffed, but the waist is not because the material is a little too heavy. Her pants are dark brown glove suede. Her long, heavy, and very straight hair is easily styled into a side bun, with lots of hairspray and a few pins.

This Black Barbie ® Doll wears a white glove-leather pantsuit here, with a small chiffon scarf tucked inside the jacket to give the appearance of a blouse. The red buckle shoes look terrific with this outfit, don't they? She is my favorite Black Barbie ® Doll, because her hair is just perfect the way it is and requires no more than a quick brush-up fluff for modeling.

Her blond working partner, the Western Barbie ® Doll, is my least favorite of all the blond dolls because her face is overpowered by the blue eye makeup and her skin tone is too pink. I'd rather be half-baked than overbaked, wouldn't you?

She is wearing another checkerboard shirt, with suede buccaneer pants. I tried brown boots before deciding on the yellow buckle shoes that pick up the color of her shirt. She is balanced against the side of the chair.

This is the Hispanic Barbie® Doll, the prettiest Barbie® Doll of recent years, in my opinion. Her long dark hair is very easy to manage and looks more like real hair than most of the others.

She is wearing a deep maroon sweater and matching hat over a pair of plain slacks made from a tiny cotton plaid I found in an old dress in a secondhand shop. You will see many other garments made from this fabric. It is a terrific lightweight 100% cotton that works very well for these tiny dolls.

This time our model wears a black glove-leather pantsuit I had a terrible time making because I wanted to preserve the stitched lines on the backs of the gloves for the front of the jacket. It finally worked out all right, but I had to hand-stitch the collar to make it fit properly.

Her hat is made from suede cloth and adds just the right finishing touch. You will find the pattern for this hat along with all the other hats in the chapter on Accessories.

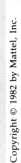

Checking Ready-made Doll Clothes

Before we get into making pants for your doll, I want you to check your commercial doll clothes. Turn them inside out so you can see the seams, hems, and darts. Most of the commercial patterns I have seen have elasticized waists on pants, so you may not see darts anywhere except in the tops of dresses and in blouses, which fit snugly over the doll's breasts. Using darts is the only way to fit material over her breasts, when both the shoulders and waist are properly fitted, unless we use stretchy fabric.

Another beautiful blonde, posed in profile this time to show her lovely hair brushed back over her shoulders as well as the nice line of the ice-blue satin jacket and the leather pants. Her little stocking cap is made from a fine polyester knit and topped with a pompon.

Elastic waists are all right for pants, but they never fit as well as those with darts; they bunch around the waist. I also think they are actually more difficult to make; managing the tiny piece of elastic is a pain in the neck (or somewhere else!), because it has to be stretched as you sew. I have never used elastic thread, though my friend Marion who spews out ideas like a popcorn machine thinks it is the best possible way.

THE PANTS

Making pants may seem complicated the first time, but I assure you they will come out right if you follow the instructions, and the second pair will be a piece of cake.

As instructed on the pattern, you will cut two pieces exactly alike by pinning the pattern to folded material. Each piece represents one side of the doll's body, *not* back and front, but left and right, which, when folded, looks like one pant leg waiting to be joined to its counterpart. That's exactly what it is.

The A edge is the front crotch and B is the back. First stitch the two pieces together along the A edge, then lay the sewn-together pieces flat, wrong-side up. The seam you see is the front center of what will soon be a completed pair of pants. The darts marked on either side of that seam should be stitched now. Then join the B edge up to the halfway mark, leaving a back opening large enough to slip over your doll's hips.

If you intend to machine-hem the pants, rather than glue or fuse, you may do that now, before matching the front and rear crotch seams, pinning them, and sewing up one leg and down the other.

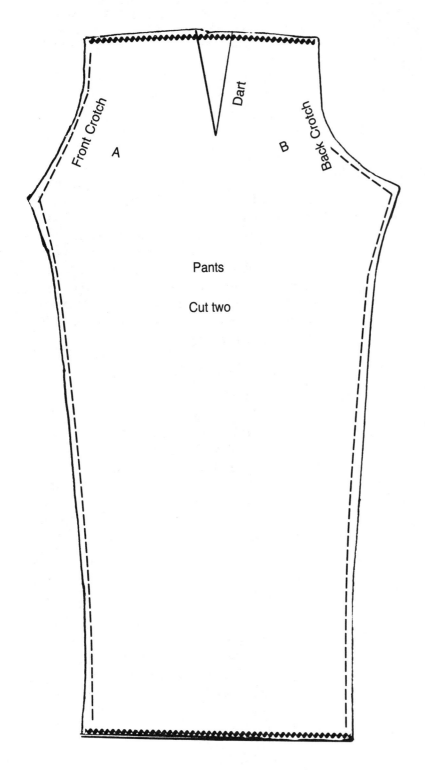

Front Crotch

Dart

Back Crotch

A

B

Pants

Cut two

PATTERN IV

▲▲▲▲▲▲▲▲▲▲▲▲▲▲▲▲▲▲▲ Seam

– – – – – – – – – – Hem

How to Finish Pants Hems

The decision on how to finish pants hems should be based entirely on the material used. As you have probably observed, I often use very thin glove leather for pants, and I always glue those hems after every bit of sewing is done. Then I turn the waistband and glue it down, too.

However, if you use fabric, and I recommend you do for at least the *first* pair of pants you make, using glue is not an option because it stiffens the fabric. Fusion tape is an option, of course, but only if you use it before sewing up the legs.

Your toothpick will be useful at this stage, no matter how you choose to finish your hems. I use it to hold the tiny hem in place as I sew, whether I'm hand-stitching or hemming on the machine or gluing or fusing.

Before making any decision about how to finish the hems, turn the pants right side out, using a crochet hook to pull the legs through. Make sure that the pants are the right length and that there is enough room in back to cover the doll's bottom when the two open edges are tacked down and a snap is attached at the waist.

A Proper Fit

I must say something at this point about fitting things to the Barbie® Doll, because if you are off just a little bit or if your fabric has zero stretch to it, you can end up with a waist that is too tight to close with a snap, or with a gap in the pants opening in back. After you make each garment a few times, your eye will tell you when it's close, but that is not very comforting as you realize that one-eighth inch more fabric would have taken care of the problem. In the case of pants, you can always open the darts and do them over, but I'm sure you would figure this out for yourself.

As for choosing fabric, I can only say that experience seems to be the best teacher. In general, heavy material just won't work because it comes out looking too bulky. Almost all the materials I use have some stretch and give to them, but the tightly woven fabrics like cotton, satin, and some of the polyesters trigger a little warning bell in my brain that says something like "pay attention, be careful!"

This lovely model shows off a pair of check pants, topped with a cowl-collared white sweater and stocking cap made from a pair of baby mittens. Perfect for a casual afternoon.

45

The Pretty Secrets Christie® Doll models a red velvet pantsuit, trimmed with lace at collar and cuffs. This is a mandarin jacket, particularly effective in this scarlet velvet, isn't it?

The Christie® Doll takes a moment from her modeling assignment. She is wearing white glove-leather pants, a red bouclé turtleneck sweater, and a red velvet beret. Note the little red wedge-heel slides.

These skirts, made from the same cotton print fabric, are modeled by the Golden Dreams Barbie® Doll on the left, who wears a simple dirndl over her white lace-trimmed tricot blouse, and the Malibu Christie® Doll on the right, who shows off a flounced prairie skirt, topped with a white velvet jacket.

The Golden Dreams Barbie® Doll and her modeling partner, the Black Barbie® Doll, walk out in two versions of velour and suede-cloth ensembles. The long-pants, worn by the Golden Dreams Barbie® Doll, are complemented by a casual sweat shirt of contrasting velour. The Black Barbie® Doll's velour-trimmed jacket maintains the softly rounded line of her knickers. Nice combinations, aren't they?

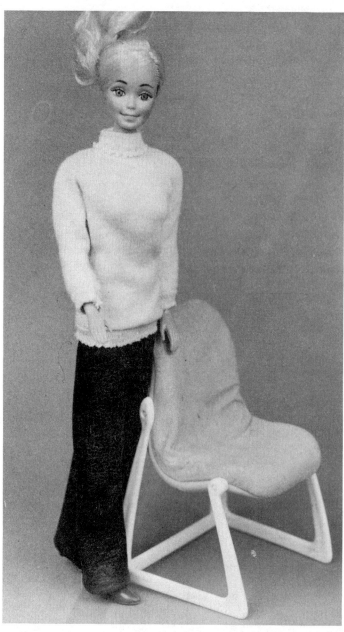

Your First Barbie ® Doll is braced against a chair to show to best advantage her long cream-colored sweat shirt with its modified turtleneck collar. She wears the shirt over a pair of smooth black leather pants. We styled her hair into a loose ponytail for this pose.

This is the Western Barbie ® Doll, ready to step out and show off her big, loose cardigan. The 100% wool pants she wears seem to be dwarfed by her heavy sweater, don't you agree?

The Black Barbie® Doll models a casual ensemble consisting of light cotton-denim pants, a powder-blue shirt-sweater, made from T-shirt cotton, with a tiny pleat front and center and topped by this sensational royal-blue smooth leather jacket, which was made from leather salvaged from a purse. Terrific, isn't it?

Fusion Tape

Now let's get on with our consideration of fusion tape as a particularly wonderful device for giving these tiny garments a really professional looking finish.

For a finished edge, fusion tape accomplishes the same purpose as hemming does, but without leaving surface stitches to show. I began using it with lamé because hand-stitching this fabric is difficult and machine stitches just look awful on the surface. I had to play around with the fusing process and ruined some fabric along the way, but I finally arrived at a foolproof way of using it.

The secret is to use a press cloth (paper towels also work nicely), so that your iron can be hot enough to make a good bond without scorching the fabric. I also found that pressing the hem edge down before applying the fusion tape made the process easier. The tape comes in a variety of widths; the narrowest I have been able to find is three-quarter inch. That's too wide, of course. We don't want our hems to be any wider than one-quarter inch, so you will cut a long, narrow strip approximately that width for starters. If you use a paper towel as a press cloth, beware of the fusion tape leaking out or overlapping the hem; it is difficult to pull paper towel bonded to fabric away from the garment. This isn't a problem if you use a press cloth made of cotton.

Once you master the use of fusion tape, you will find other uses for it, but above all, don't get discouraged while learning how to make it work. I am the world's worst klutz, and I got it together, so *anyone* can! Practicing is a smart thing to do before you actually use it on an almost-finished garment.

Gluing Hems

As discussed earlier, I use glue to hem leather and ultrasuede. There is a bit of a knack to using glue for this purpose. After trying leather glue (which is very runny and bonds very quickly), Elmer's and other white

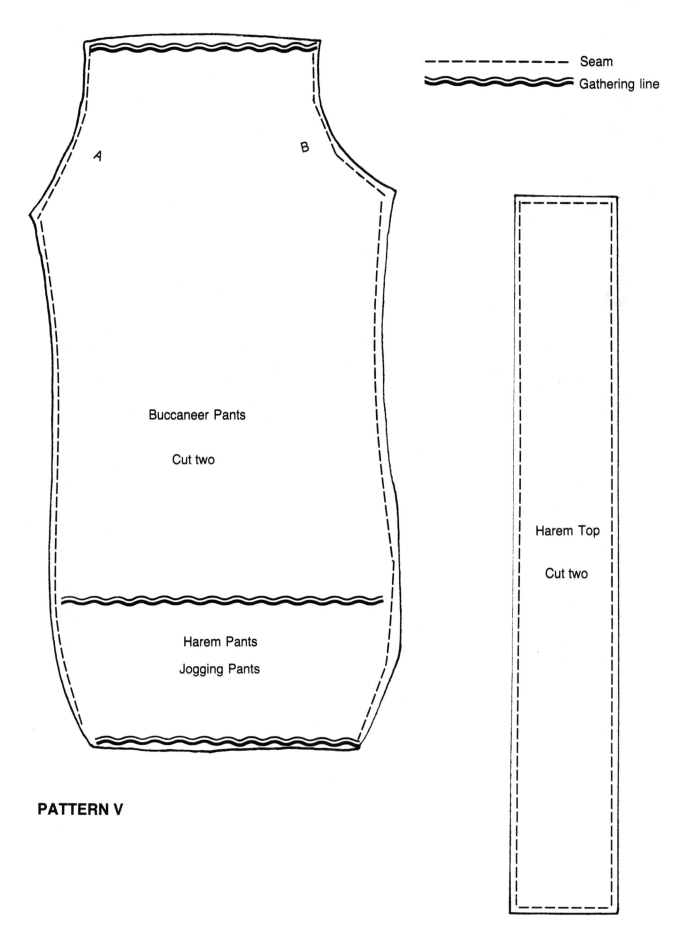

- - - - - Seam
〰〰〰 Gathering line

A   B

Buccaneer Pants

Cut two

Harem Pants

Jogging Pants

Harem Top

Cut two

PATTERN V

50 ———

glues (which don't bond quickly enough to suit me), and some of the quick-bonding wonder glues, I found out that nothing beats rubber cement. It bonds neither too fast nor too slowly and is much easier to control because of its thick, gummy quality. It spreads nicely with a toothpick if you use a minimal amount. I found that the finished product is uniformly better with rubber cement. You can apply just enough pressure to bond the glue to both sides if you hold it together with your fingers for a few moments, but you can also use a paperweight, a paper clip, a clothespin, or an alligator clamp. Hair clips will also hold the edges together until the glue sets. I do it this way when I am making several pairs of pants at the same time and they are all ready at once to be hem-glued.

HAREM AND JOGGING PANTS, BUCCANEER PANTS/KNICKERS

You will see that all these pants are simple variations of the regular pants pattern. They are wider in the leg, but are assembled in exactly the same way, except for gathering the ankle edge or the bottom edge that comes just below the knee in the buccaneer pants/knickers, instead of hemming. You can attach a small cuff (it's almost too tiny to bother with) after gathering, or you can dispense with the cuff and simply gather the edge. I don't like dealing with elastic, but rather just pull the thread tightly and then stitch over the gathers to secure them. When I use a cuff, I pleat rather than gather. It is less bulky, and the cuff goes on more neatly.

The top for the jogging suit is simply a cardigan worn backward, with loose gathers around neck, sleeves, and waist. The special top for harem pants is very simple to make. It is two long strips, each a bit wider in the middle than at the ends, which are hemmed or fused all around. The two strips are then joined at the midpoint between the doll's breasts, pulled over her shoulders, and tied at the neck. The other two ends are tied around the waist. As a special touch, I like to drape a loose shawl over this harem top, but it isn't really necessary.

Our model takes a stroll in her deep maroon terry-cloth jog suit trimmed with bands of dusty rose suede cloth. Her white clogs don't offer enough support for a healthy jog.

The Happy Birthday Barbie® Doll, with her long, golden hair flowing back over her shoulders, displays a rust-colored suede-cloth jogging suit, or leisure suit, if you prefer that designation. She certainly couldn't be expected to do much jogging in her little white slides, could she?

These joggers are standing free with the help of a tiny piece of floral clay on their forward shoes. Actually, part of the balance is achieved by leaning them into each other. After a hard run, they hold each other up.

Their jogging suits are made from a nubbly polyester fabric, piped in contrasting colors. The tops are backward cardigans, very easy to make by turning under the neck edge and topstitching the piping, and the pants are plain old everyday harem pants.

The Black Barbie® Doll wears a creamy white suit piped in red, and the Happy Birthday Barbie® Doll shows off her royal-blue suit piped in white. They both wear proper running shoes, of course.

The Malibu Christie® Doll perches on the edge of a wicker table as she waits her turn to show off this royal-blue knicker suit. The suit is made of lightweight suede cloth, which shapes nicely into the turtleneck overblouse with a narrow cuff around the bottom that complements the cuffed knickers.

Here's another look at Your First Barbie® Doll sitting on the wicker settee. She models her deep purple velvet jacket over a pair of cotton print knickers with a dark, plum-colored background covered with tiny pink and white blossoms. A practical ensemble for an easy day.

Chapter Three

Haute Couture

ET'S TALK ABOUT high fashion, or what is called *haute couture* in France. Obviously, high fashion means just exactly what it says: the absolute ultimate in the fashion world. If we glance through some current fashion magazines like *Vogue* or *Harper's Bazaar* or *Glamour* or *Mademoiselle*, we quickly note that there seems to be a general consensus of opinion on what constitutes high fashion in this country and what is really hot this season. The slick magazines are all showing the same kinds of dresses, pants, coats, and jackets.

Street dresses are very feminine and pretty this year, made of beautiful fabrics and trimmed with embroidery and lace. The harshly tailored lines of earlier fashion seasons have noticeably softened into rounder, curvier lines.

I am just knocked out by the smashing blouses, especially the silk ones in all the gorgeous, jewel colors of the rainbow. Shopping for *a* blouse is an exercise in futility for me; I always have a terrible time making a choice because of the profusion of colors and designs.

Pants come in every imaginable material, from cotton all the way through solid metallics and Lurex, which is a stretchy fabric with a gold or silver thread running throughout. Not only are pants being shown in all these exotic

materials, but they come in some very exotic shapes as well. Harem pants and knickers are seen everywhere, for daytime and nighttime, in every possible combination of fabric and color.

Coats, jackets, capes, stoles, shawls—everything we've ever dreamed of wearing is being shown in the slicks, a positive embarrassment of riches in stunning furs, velvets, brocades, laces, and satins. There is something for everyone—your taste can scarcely be too far-out.

I have attempted to leave no stone unturned in my quest to dress the Barbie® Dolls in examples of all these gorgeous things. Without a pang of conscience I have stolen from every designer line that has turned my head.

Personal Taste

Let's consider personal taste for a moment, and what forms and shapes our individual tastes for what we wear.

Because I am a very small person (5 feet tall, 100 pounds, small frame) who wears size three or four in adult clothes, and size fourteen in children's clothes, my options are more limited than those of a woman 5'6" who weighs between 115 and 130 pounds. Children's clothes? Of course! I've worn boys' jeans for years and a few years ago when blazers became such a hot item, I started wearing boys' jackets, too.

The Hippie Movement captured my kids' imaginations in the mid-1960s and when they started wearing hippie clothes and telling me how square I was in my little whipped-cream dresses, I had to consider the merit (or lack thereof) in limiting myself to the buttons, bows, and ruffles of cutesy little-girl clothes on a grown woman. I discussed my questions with a dear friend named Kay Pace, whose kids were roughly the same ages as mine. We were having lots of discussions about our adolescent kids then, but this was a new departure.

Kay knew a lot more about fashion than I did, and she suggested that I toss out all the cutesy (her word) clothes I owned and that I go for a more tailored look. The idea of throwing out all my pretty dresses was shocking at first, but as I started buying shirtwaists and fairly plain A-line dresses, I began to see that she really knew what she was talking about. I kept all my frilly blouses and decided that was the one place I could pig out on buttons, bows, ruffles, and lace.

Kay also advised me to get rid of anything pastel colored. "You need primary colors," she said. That took longer because I adore soft, pastel colors, but she was right. If I needed to have soft colors around me, she said, use them in wallpaper and upholstery.

So we can all agree that my taste is basically conservative. I would love to be able to wear the kinds of things taller women can get away with, but I learned even before Kay told me about cutesy clothes that if I wear anything printed or patterned, it must be a tiny print or pattern—never, never can I wear big, splashy flowers or geometrics. Small people just can't pull it off. We end up looking like an unfinished canvas, with all the colors running off the edges.

This Barbie® Doll poses in a wool suit piped in matching suede cloth. Her belt buckle is taken off a watchband—perfect scale! The cordovan boots were painted with mulberry nail polish.

This beautiful blond doll, whose hair has been coiled around her head, models a daytime dress of 100% cotton in a tiny plaid. The dress is a variation of the basic blouse pattern (rounded scoop neck) attached to a nine-inch-wide skirt, softly pleated. Neck and sleeve edges are bound with white cotton bias tape to give the professionally finished look that every dress designer strives for. Sensational, easy-care dress!

The Italian Barbie® Doll displays a very high-fashion outfit: A beautiful mink coat tops her eggshell glove-leather suit. Very smart and dainty brown slides finish this picture of ultrahigh fashion.

The Golden Dreams Barbie® Doll holds the pose for the photographer to catch her cinnamon, dyed-chinchilla coat with matching hat. Her dark brown suede pants add glamour to this stunning ensemble.

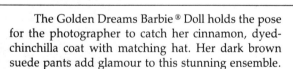

The Scottish Barbie® Doll models another version of the daytime dress. This fabric is pure silk in a tiny pattern that is perfect for the purposes of any designer of these miniature clothes. Sleeve cuffs and neck binding are of red rayon bias tape as is the narrow waistband, a color accent that picks up the red in the basic print. Isn't this model a knockout?

The Parisian Barbie® Doll sits in the wings, awaiting her turn to show the pleated plain-weave skirt worn with a velvet blazer and boots.

Fashion Versus Style

If we distinguish between fashion and style, we might say that fashion is for everyone, while style is our individual way of applying fashion to the dimensions and limitations our personal genetic heritage has given us.

Growing up little (sounds like a book title, doesn't it?) taught me to scale my desires down to the realm of possibility, but in my secret heart I always wanted to be tall and willowy. After all, what woman in her right mind would opt for cute as the ultimate compliment? Cute is less than thrilling after age twenty-five.

What about chic and what about haute couture? Well, we can all be chic if we are very careful. And we can certainly aspire to haute couture as well, if we remember our limitations. That's the whole point of finding out what our style is. Learning what it *isn't* may be one of the most important things we ever do.

A fashion-conscious woman who knows her own style and her own body can see at a glance whether she will be able to wear everything (or indeed anything) in a given designer line. Few of us have figures like the models in the slick magazines, so the clothes that look so wonderful on tall, skinny women will probably look awful on us, unless we make the necessary concessions to the shape God gave us.

The Idealized Figure

We can stay comfortably in fantasyland, however, as long as we are making clothes for the Barbie® Doll, whose figure is highly idealized even in comparison with such famous fashion models as Lauren Hutton and Cheryl Tiegs. Whatever we would like to believe to the contrary, Barbie® is not your average, all-American girl. Her legs are too long in proportion to the rest of her body, and her waist is much too small for an athletic, sporty, all-American girl. Her bosom is very pretty, but larger than life.

However, she is undoubtedly an ideal, for which we can all be grateful as we attempt to turn her into our dream of high fashion. She can wear with panache all the haute couture clothes of this year, or any other year for that matter. For our purposes as amateur dress designers, her idealized figure is simply wonderful; everything we create will look fantastic if we keep within the proper scale for her. Pants look sensational precisely because of those disproportionately long legs. All our dresses and blouses will look terrific if they hang well from her shoulders and fit well over her bosom. Actually, with a figure like hers, we'd all look fine in rags and tatters.

But we aren't interested in dressing our doll in rags and tatters. Since she represents (in part, at least) our vision of the way we'd like to look in clothes, we must keep in mind the fact that her figure is not something we can realistically hope to achieve for ourselves. Even if we were willing to wear a Merry Widow waist cincher like Scarlett O'Hara, subjecting ourselves to a case of the vapors for lack of oxygen to our brains, we still couldn't fake those long, long legs, could we? High heels may be fashionable and stylish, but stilts haven't made it to *Vogue* yet.

It Ain't Easy!

That was my family's catch phrase for anything that was a little too much like work to be fun. I think it started when my son was about three years old and I was looking for a good persuader/motivator to make him pick up his toys and hide them in the big toy chest that stood empty in a corner of the kids' bedroom while toys were strewn through every room of the house.

Explaining to him that cleaning house didn't thrill me any more than picking up toys did him, I said, "It's just work or even slave labor; there's no intrinsic value in being tidy, but it makes everyone's life easier and more pleasant. It ain't easy, but it's necessary!"

From that time on, we all said "It ain't easy" for anything that was just work, just drudgery, just a pain in the neck. Somehow over the years it was used more to characterize five-minute jobs that *were* easy.

Patterns, Fashion Conformity, and Simplicity

The patterns for the clothes in this chapter were designed with two main considerations in mind. First, of course, I have tried to meet the current craze for prettiness, with the soft emphasis on the beauty of the female figure. The dresses and blouses are very feminine, even frothy in their reliance on gorgeous fabrics and trims. Lots of lace and embroidery, sensational colors, and perfect fit are the most important elements of the finished garments. The suits shown are softened by pretty, very feminine blouses and scarves. The suit patterns are straightforward and simple, with lots of room for variation. As in all patterns in this book, I encourage you to spread out and use your imaginations to improve on basic designs.

The secondary consideration is simplicity and ease of execution. Because these patterns are so tiny, I have made them just as simple as I could, with an absolute minimum of darts and other fitting complications. In fact, I will gratefully welcome suggestions from other pattern-makers on ways of simplifying further.

Fitting Problems

Perfect fit can be a problem with dresses and blouses because they must be open either in front or in back in order to get them on and off our doll without mussing her hair. I prefer back openings for everything, including the blouse with the bow at the neck, because finishing the edges of a fitted blouse that closes in front is a formidable problem. It is much easier to have back closures that look neat, simply because our doll's back is a whole lot flatter than her front. It ain't easy!

The blouse pattern is also the bodice pattern for the dress. The most difficult part of the blouse is the sleeves or the lack thereof. If you opt for a sleeveless blouse or dress, you still must bind the edge of the armholes, which is a delicate job at best. And if you use the sleeves, you must be very careful when setting them into the armhole. I always baste sleeves in before I do the final stitching, and

even then I keep my handy-dandy toothpick nearby for pushing the fabric along as I stitch. To make full sleeves, you simply add one-quarter inch to each side of the sleeve when you cut it out and then ease the fabric into the armhole as you stitch.

The skirt of the dress is pleated or gathered (I prefer tiny pleats) to four inches before attaching the bodice. I prefer pleating to gathering because it is more precise, and God knows, there are real difficulties in precision when working with such diminutive pieces.

The wool skirts are easy to make and will turn out right every time if you follow the

The Hispanic Barbie® and Kissing Barbie® Dolls meet before their strolls down the models' aisle. The Hispanic Barbie® Doll displays a rather formal black linen suit with a traditional white bow-tie blouse. The Kissing Barbie® Doll models a wine-colored outfit: plain-weave wool slacks and coordinating suede-cloth jacket. Her blouse with a small self-tie is made from a light silk scarf.

The Hispanic Barbie® Doll demonstrates a beautiful white silk dress made from a border print scarf. It is rather stiff material, so when the skirt is tightly pleated, it stands out quite effectively. Her sandals have been painted with a pale mauve nail polish to match.

A pure silk dress with a tiny print is modeled here by the Ballet Barbie® Doll. This dress is made with the pajama pattern, piped and belted with a matching red bias tape, and worn with red sandals, of course.

Your First Barbie® Doll models a soft, suede-cloth version of the pajama adaptation. Trimmed with a dainty narrow lace, this dress should have less fullness in the front panel, or it should be belted. Falling from the high yoke, it could almost be a maternity dress.

The Golden Dreams Christie® Doll's hair has been drawn straight back and coiled to show all the auburn hair around her face; that color hair matches the beautiful mural print on her dress. This is a fine delicate pure silk, finished at the neck and cuffs with the same fabric. There is no belt, which would only distract from the beauty of the fabric.

The Christie® Doll wears a lush short mink coat. Her rust-colored hat matches the knickers of soft suede cloth, cuffed just above her boots. Isn't she pretty?

A very old Barbie® Doll, this model was probably manufactured in the early 1960s. She poses here in a black linen skirt accented with a very stiff taffeta jacket, which is a basic dull black with gold pinstripes. The taffeta is difficult to drape, and I wasn't at all sure it would work out for the tiny models, but apparently I did everything right in shaping and cutting the material.

with a contrasting color to relieve the boredom of a solid color jacket melting into the same-color skirt or pants.

BLOUSES AND SHIRTS

So let's get on with some talk about the blouse. I love the pattern because it is almost fail-safe and because it is amenable to many variations. You can change the shape of the neckline, make sleeves of any shape or length you prefer, and use any lightweight fabric.

My favorite is the tucked, fine white cotton blouse that you'll see in this chapter. I like it especially, because I didn't have to do the tucking myself. It is made from an old blouse of mine that was beginning to wear thin around the collar and underarms, but that I saved for just this purpose. It is very fine, thin white cotton, absolutely perfect for anything we want to make for our dolls, and it is the simplest execution of the blouse pattern, too; sleeveless, with the armholes and neckline bound with untucked fabric from the same blouse.

The blouse pattern is, as you can see, just one piece if you opt for no sleeves. Darts are marked both at the sides and at the bottom edge of the blouse front. You have the choice of using either or both, but if you don't use "up" darts, you must take in the sides at the waist to compensate for the fabric allowed for darts. I found it difficult to tuck the blouse into skirts and pants, so I have just shown it as an overblouse to avoid bunchiness around the waist. One more reminder of the importance of using very fine, thin materials.

I also use the pajama/nightgown pattern (see Chapter Four, Lingerie) for making dresses, and it is certainly adaptable for blouses as well. Just make the pajama top from your blouse fabric and incorporate any changes from the basic pattern, such as a cowl

directions carefully. The hems are all fused and the pleats are pressed in before sewing up the back of the skirt. All the skirts have a mid-back closure, so there won't be a seam on the side to change the line of the skirt.

In addition to the wonderfully light wools, I discovered a very light suede cloth that *is* a synthetic, but that just can't be beat for softness and flexibility. It fits and drapes perfectly, because its fine texture borders on limpness, which is exactly what we need and want for a really excellent fit. It comes in a wide variety of colors, and for all I know, it might even be available in some prints. I have seen only solid colors, so I edge the jackets collar or modified turtleneck. A V-neck won't work because the yoke isn't deep enough, but a small mandarin collar does work, and a narrow row of gathered lace looks sensational, as you can see on some of the pajama pictures.

Cutting out and finishing the blouse is very simple. Pin the pattern to your material, cut around the pattern carefully, then follow the instructions on the pattern for finishing.

If you are making a sleeveless blouse with a plain neckline, you should bind the armholes, the neck, and/or the collar *before* sewing up the sides of the blouse. You can do it after sewing, but I find it easier to finish the openings on a flat piece of fabric. Don't forget to put in the darts first.

If you want sleeves, cut them out and pin them to the armholes. I fold the sleeve the long way to determine the exact middle at the top where it is set into the armhole, and pin it there. Then I baste it into the armhole, easing sleeve fabric into the given space, before sewing it on the machine. Remember, right sides of fabric together here!

If I want a gathered-at-the-wrist sleeve, I do that as the next step, or I sew on a cuff instead of simple gathers, then the darts, and finally, the sides and inside sleeve seam on each side of the blouse.

This operation is exactly the same, whether you are making a blouse or a dress top. And don't be discouraged if it doesn't work out perfectly the very first time. These items are very tiny, and your attempts at precision will get easier after you've made a few.

PATTERN VI

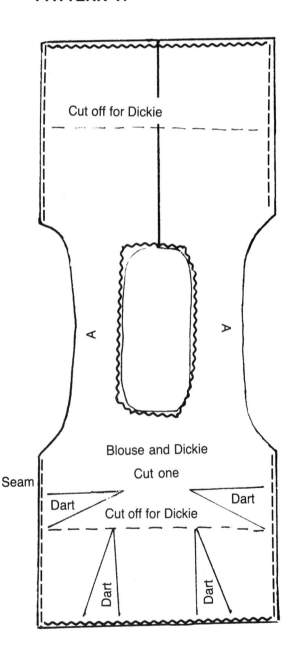

Hem

Cut two

Sleeve

A

Cut off for Dickie

A

A

Blouse and Dickie

Cut one

Seam

Dart   Dart

Cut off for Dickie

Dart   Dart

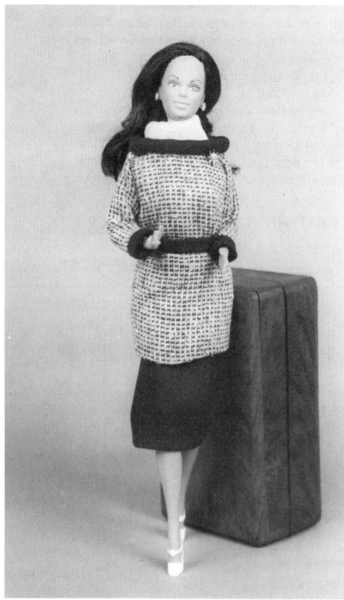

The Italian Barbie® Doll walks out in a sensational-looking tunic dress of a soft lightweight wool, trimmed with the same heavier dark brown wool of her straight skirt. The tunic is set off by the little starburst brooch worn just below the wide cowl collar of dark rich brown wool. Under her tunic she wears a soft cream-colored dickie. Isn't she *très chic?*

This pale green glove-leather pantsuit, modeled by the Parisian Barbie® Doll, is a perfect example of what can be accomplished with a pair of gloves and careful fitting. The collar and cuffs are reversed to show the suede side of the leather. Her dickie is made from a dark paisley cotton velvet print, a lovely contrast to the flat green leather.

The Golden Dreams Christie® Doll, whose hair has been brushed straight back and then brought forward to cover the roots, models a white tricot blouse softly edged with zigzag stitching around the neckline and sleeves. The red flower-printed dirndl would look sensational with any white blouse. Her necklace is there to point up the nice line of the scoop neck.

The Ballet Barbie® Doll demonstrates the basic dress pattern in a very fine sheer cotton, trimmed with a flounce at neckline and around the hem, with push-up, very full sleeves.

THE TUNIC DRESS

This is a very simple pattern of two pieces, one for the front and one for the back, or if cut on a fold across the shoulder line, just one piece. The back must be split in either case.

The tunic, as you can see from the photos, is worn over a narrow skirt of the same fabric or of fabric that matches the trim on the tunic. While I have not shown any examples of tunics worn over pants in this collection, I have tried them with straight pants and with knickers, and they are perfectly delightful.

This is one of my favorite haute couture patterns, probably because I resisted making it right up to the end of getting the collection together. For some reason I thought it would be difficult to make and to shape to the model's figure, but it turned out to be one of the simplest patterns of all.

The skirt should be very narrow and absolutely straight, and I have made an exception to my rule against elasticized waists in this case to avoid darts. Use your own judgment on this issue; try it both ways, perhaps, to see which one you prefer.

I caution you to use very soft, flexible material for the tunic because of the nature of the pattern. Anything remotely stiff will create folds in the sleeves, and the success of this garment really depends on a nice smooth line.

I have used very soft wool for two of the tunics shown and regret that I didn't have time to make one from glove leather, which I feel certain would look absolutely wonderful.

As you see from the pattern, it shows a simple rounded neckline, but I urge you to try something different. Two of my tunics have little rolled collars that give the impression of a modified boat neck, but you could choose a deeper rounded line that would look like a scoop neck, or, of course, a V-line.

Good luck with this pattern.

The Golden Dreams Barbie ® Doll steps out in a smart tunic dress made of a very lightweight 100% wool. The tunic would look just as terrific over a pair of solid brown leather pants. Her hat and belt are made of a very soft shiny leather, accented by off-white pipe cleaner chenille glued directly to the leather. Please note her little starburst brooch on the rolled collar. This brooch is actually a single post earring. This ensemble is the very essence of haute couture, don't you agree?

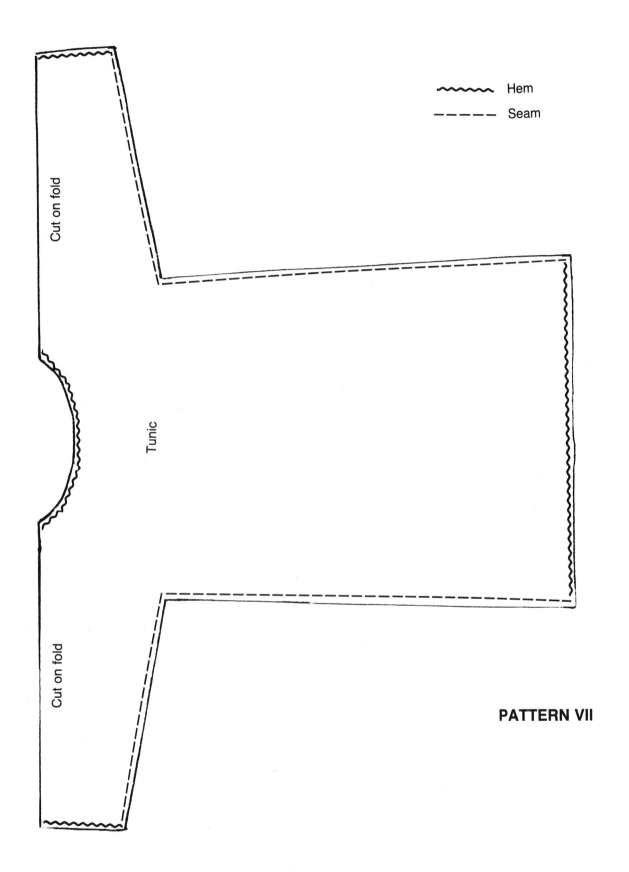

Hem

Seam

Cut on fold

Tunic

Cut on fold

PATTERN VII

The Happy Birthday Barbie® Doll poses in a black Persian lamb coat trimmed with lush mink. Her eggshell-colored tricot pants add some light to this picture.

A pale pink and silver Lurex jacket points up the delicate parchment leather of the Parisian Barbie® Doll's pants. Her pale pink sandals complete this stunning outfit.

The Hawaiian Barbie® Doll's downward gaze emphasizes her little knit hat, which tops her gray flannel coat, accented with cuffed sleeves and a self-belt. The lace-trimmed, scarlet velvet blouse adds a nice touch of color.

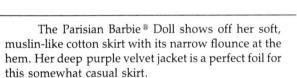

The Parisian Barbie® Doll shows off her soft, muslin-like cotton skirt with its narrow flounce at the hem. Her deep purple velvet jacket is a perfect foil for this somewhat casual skirt.

THE SKIRTS

We will start with the most difficult skirt—the pleated all-around skirt—instead of with the easier ones. That way you'll go to the simpler skirts with cool confidence once you've demonstrated to your own satisfaction that making a pleated all-around skirt isn't actually all that complicated.

As with everything else in this book, I recommend that you practice pleating before you actually begin making this skirt. If you have some extra material, use it first as a trial run. Pleated skirts aren't really hard; they merely require a little extra-special care and precision.

My mother-in-law taught me how to pin pleats to the ironing board cover many years ago, as she watched me struggle with an accordion-pleated skirt. Frankly, that was one of the most important lessons I learned from her.

Pressing and Pleating

We begin with a piece of material 16½ inches by 5¼ inches. Fuse or hem it first, making your hem no deeper than ¼ inch. If you choose to hem it, you should press the hem flat before you start on the pleats. I pin my fabric to the ironing board, using straight pins stuck in at a slight angle, then begin making ¼-inch pleats, sticking a pin into each end of each pleat to secure it firmly to the ironing board cover. When I have five or six nice straight pleats tightly anchored to the board, I press them with a fairly hot iron and a damp press cloth to get really sharp pleats. I have used paper towels for a press cloth, but only with cotton. Wool requires more heat than cotton when pleating, so a press cloth works better. Of course, you can also use a steam iron if you are very careful to keep your fingers out of the way.

On balance, I prefer a light press cloth over paper towel and/or steam iron, because it is easier to direct the moisture exactly where I want it without unnecessarily wetting the unpleated fabric. I pull out the pins as I go along, but replace the last two before continuing with the next batch of pleats. We repeat this process until the entire piece of fabric is pleated, leaving a narrow, flat strip at the end for the skirt closure.

Before attaching the waistband, I always stitch along the top edge where the waistband will cover my stitches in order to firmly anchor the pleats below (see below). After attaching your waistband, try the skirt on your doll to make sure it goes all the way around her waist.

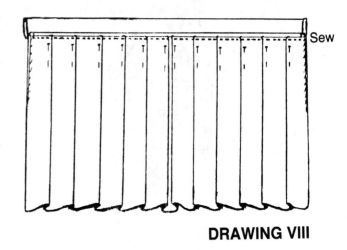

DRAWING VIII

Don't Panic

If it's too big, don't panic! You can simply cut off the excess material. If it is too small, you shouldn't panic either; your skirt is still salvageable. The pleats are probably a little too wide, and you can press them flat and start over. Don't be discouraged if you have to do things over; every seamstress in the world will make an occasional miscalculation or an outright mistake, but I (through millions of mistakes) have learned that you rarely have to discard fabric and start over from scratch if you sit down, be calm, and think about where you went wrong and whether you can salvage your work.

As mentioned earlier, I use only back closures for the skirts to avoid spoiling the line of the skirt with a side seam. If you make a kilt skirt, with a safety pin on the front, you may have to check out a side closure. I haven't shown a kilt because I just haven't come up with a tiny enough tartan plaid.

Kick-pleat or inverted-pleat skirts are

made very easily by pressing in the pleats right down the center of the little modified circle skirt, front and back, and finishing with tiny invisible stitches to hold the pleats in place, stitching from the wrong side of your material.

Cutting and Sewing Leather

As you can see, I have shown a glove-leather suit with skirt, along with the green kid pantsuit. So let's talk about the special handling of leather now. These instructions will be repeated in Chapter Six on Fur and Leather.

First, I *always* draw my pattern directly on leather, because if it is pinned, the pinhole will stay there. When cutting out the drawn pattern, I cut just inside the line; just barely inside, so those marks are gone before I start sewing. Glove leather, which I use more than any other leather, is easy to cut with any pair of sharp scissors.

Using Old Gloves

I have been buying kid gloves from secondhand stores for several years and have even considered contacting glove manufacturers to ask if they would sell their seconds (gloves with a small flaw or mistake) to me. I buy mostly long, over-the-elbow gloves, because there is enough leather in them to make an entire pantsuit or a jacket and a skirt.

The Scottish Barbie ® Doll models an ensemble of white kid-glove leather. This suit and matching hat are made from two pairs of gloves, the red-braid-trimmed gloves were only wrist length, which is just about enough leather for a jacket, if very carefully cut. So I used another pair to make the skirt. The kick pleat is simply ironed into place with a cool iron and, of course, a press cloth, then secured from the inside with tiny invisible-on-the-surface stitches.

There is no pattern for the jacket made of glove leather because each pair of gloves is different, and we have to use them the way they are made. Many have long wrist openings; if they end very close to the thumb, they make it imperative to use the opening for the front of the jacket. You can always bind the edge with a long narrow strip from leftovers, and in fact, you can even use leather from a different pair of gloves, because it is all right to have a contrast in the binding. When I use a contrast here, I carry it over into cuffs for the sleeves as well.

If there is enough space between the opening and the inset stitching around the thumb,

The high sheen of this stretchy nylon gives it the look of a silk pantsuit. The jacket is made from the hand portion of a pair of gloves, utilizing the thumbs for sleeves. The pants are cut from the long, wide end of the gloves and are a lovely jewel shade of teal blue—almost turquoise. The little stand-away mandarin collar emphasizes the uniquely stiff but drapable qualities of this fabric. Stunning, isn't it?

on the end of the long flat piece, cut it out, and set it aside.

To cut out the jacket, you must first trim off all the fingers individually so that you can get as close to the upper stitching as possible, leaving the thumbs intact, but trimming down into the first finger, which is right under the thumb, to salvage as much leather as possible. Don't discard any of your scraps: the fingers can be split later to make a hat or a belt.

I cut above the top of the thumb inset about an inch, and last of all, I carefully trim off the end of the thumb, leaving an opening big enough to slide the doll's hand through. Once you have done this with both gloves, and have your doll's arms into the thumb-sleeves, you can figure out which should be the front and proceed to trim off extra material, carefully considering how much you are going to need for the back seam.

Drape and Plan

Plan carefully before you make any further cuts, but you will be able to see now how the leather can be rolled and shaped to make a collar, and how you will have to finish the front edges. When I make a completely separate collar, I often reverse the leather and use the suede side for contrast. You can also make tiny cuffs for the sleeves and fake slash pockets.

we can use that edge for the back, especially if there is some pretty stitching on the back of the hand that we would like to show on the front of our little jacket.

The thumbs are the sleeves, of course, in case you haven't guessed. They are interchangeable for right arm or left arm of the doll, depending on what we want to show on the jacket front.

Splitting Gloves

We split the glove along the outside where the seam is, right down to the end of the little finger. Then lay both gloves flat, right sides together, and draw the pants (or skirt) pattern

Think Glue

Remember that glue is extremely useful when you are working with leather. You can get leather glue from any leather shop or hardware store—perhaps even from a cobbler. You can also use rubber cement, which I prefer because it is much easier to manage than runny, very-quick-to-adhere leather glue. Rubber cement is easy to spread with a toothpick, which won't work at all with a runny kind of glue. All the glues work. Even good-old-standby Elmer's will get the job done, but why not use the best if you can get it? Don't try to glue where seams will have stretch and pull on them, but only for hems or attaching pockets, cuffs, etc.

Sewing Leather

You will need a special leather, or glove, needle, whether you are sewing by hand or by machine. Called leather needles, or glovers, they can be found in small packages just like regular ones and are carried by most yardage stores. I have even bought them in the five-and-dime. They have flat triangular tips rather than the rounded tips on ordinary needles, and are used also for sewing fur.

I make all the leather garments on my sewing machine, but I suppose, if you have enough patience, they could be done entirely by hand. You will need a good strong thimble to push your needle through the leather if you do it by hand.

Making Suits

You can use any variation you like for making wool suits for your dolls. And, of course, you are not limited to chasing down lightweight wools; you can use cotton (which pleats more easily and more sharply than any other fabric), or suede cloth, glove leather, gabardine, silk, brocade, and certainly the wool-synthetic mixes available.

I have not submitted a suit pattern along with this chapter, because the basic jacket pattern belongs in the outerwear section (see Chapter Seven) and can be combined with any of the skirts as a matter of personal preference. The circle skirt pattern is here, and the directions for making a pleated skirt preclude any need for a pattern.

When I begin to make a suit, I usually figure out exactly what kind and color blouse or shirt I will make to go with it, but sometimes I have already made something that will work perfectly with the fabric and color of the suit.

The Scottish Barbie ® Doll leans against a jewelry box stood on end here, as she prepares to walk out in a black linen suit worn over a powder-blue shirt-sweater with a stand-up collar. A classic black suit is, of course, basic to any well-ordered wardrobe for the fashion-conscious woman.

75

The Oriental Barbie® Doll models a pleated wool skirt topped by a nubbly-knit cardigan sweater. Both these garments are basic to any well-coordinated fall or winter wardrobe and can be worn separately or together in a number of combinations. A string of colored beads would liven up the sweater, and bangle bracelets could point up sleeve detail, couldn't they? The brown walking boots are a perfect finishing touch for this outfit.

The Oriental Barbie® Doll models another version of the wool suit trimmed here with a very dark brown, tightly woven wool. Her mink hat and brown boots add just the right finishing touch, don't you agree?

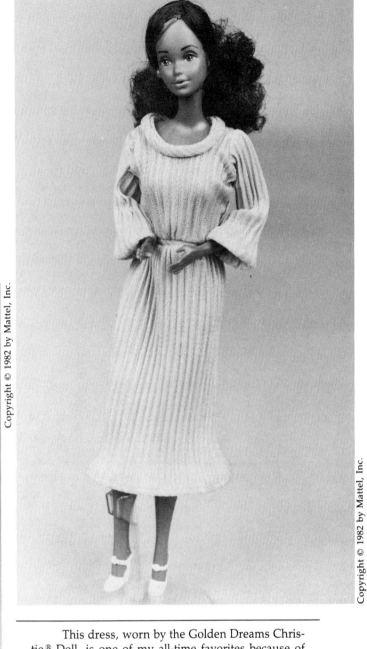

This dress, worn by the Golden Dreams Christie ® Doll, is one of my all-time favorites because of the fabric. It is tricot, knit in such a way as to produce ribs that appear to be accordion pleats. Because it is a very stretchy knit, I inserted a bias-cut waistband between the top and the skirt. How do you like the modified cowl collar and the slightly belled sleeves?

This plaid suit, worn by the Happy Birthday Barbie ® Doll, is just a bit too open a plaid for the tiny model, but the navy blue wool jacket, piped in the same plaid, is delightful, isn't it?

The Happy Birthday Barbie® Doll waits her turn to show off this outfit, which consists of a jacket made of a soft magenta velour and trimmed with a lacy collar, and a gathered 100% cotton dirndl skirt. This multipurpose combination could do double duty as a very comfortable outfit for the office and a dinner date after work.

The Christie® Doll sits for a moment in another plaid version of our basic suit. This one is trimmed with white glove leather around all the strategic edges.

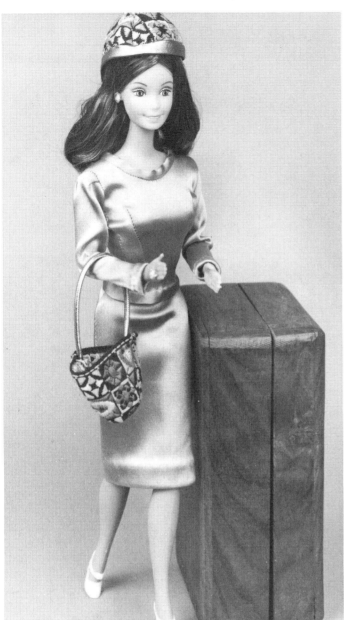

Isn't this a sensational ensemble? The beautiful Scottish model, whose red hair is arranged in a classic pageboy style, walks out in a two-piece, precisely fitted dress made from a pair of stretchy nylon gloves. This is wonderful fabric to work with, but I have not seen it in yardage stores. The observer will note that the sleeves have been very carefully set in with tiny pleats at the shoulder to make them stand out a bit—just a *tiny* bit—and that the darts at the bosom have been extended right over the bosom to ensure a perfect fit. The hat and bag are constructed from a gorgeous medallion braid that was wide enough to preserve the medallions by careful cutting. They are trimmed with gold lamé. I love it!

The Beautiful Black Barbie ® Doll awaits her turn to parade in this phenomenal brocade and lamé pantsuit. Made from the standard pants and jacket patterns, this outfit is just sensational for making an entrance to a party, isn't it? A real head-turner! The brocade was rescued from a friend's throw-away pile of old clothes. I've long since gotten used to being called a ragpicker!

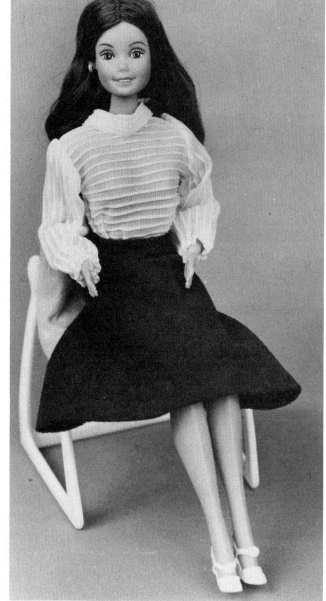

This Barbie® Doll sits on the little wicker settee, wearing a white T-shirt cotton turtleneck sweater over her brown wool pleated skirt. When she stands, her skirt covers the top of her laced boots. This combination is drawn from her large assortment of blouse, sweater, and skirt separates—mix-and-match garments that are essential to a well-balanced wardrobe for any and every season.

In a Miss Universe contest, this Miss Scotland would certainly be a contender, wouldn't she? Here she models a blouse made from an adult-human-size shirt of tucked fabric; some kind of synthetic. Wonderful fabric for making miniature clothes, this very sheer material requires minimal effort. I used a ball-point needle on my machine and very small stitches; otherwise it is almost like working with cotton. Her modified circle skirt is made of a burgundy suede cloth, which is very soft and flexible.

I hope this chapter has kindled your interest in haute couture. None of us is born with a full-blown instinct for high fashion, but all of us can learn. There are books in the library and in bookstores; if you are really interested in design and fabric, you can learn from specialized books on needlecraft, which are available in yardage stores, bookstores, and libraries.

The Parisian Barbie® Doll wears a soft, chocolate-brown suede sleeveless blouse to complement her dark brown wool pants. The multichain necklace (homemade, of course) adds just the right finishing touch to an otherwise severe neckline. Charming effect, don't you agree?

A stunning blond model shows to maximum advantage this very smart metallic fabric evening ensemble. The elbow-length sleeves on her jacket have turn-back cuffs, and there is a rather wider-than-usual continuous collar all around the front of this jacket, which could be dressed up with a scarf or a dickie. Don't you just love the matching headband?

Chapter Four

Lingerie

*M*AKING LINGERIE for the Barbie® Doll really underscores the importance of being able to sew a fine seam. Especially when making camisoles, they are almost as fast to sew by hand as by machine because the garments are so tiny. Just two little wisps of tricot (pronounced *tree-co*), with seams on each side and whatever lacy trims you may care to add.

I have shown one bra only, with half slips, but no pattern for the bras. My reason (or excuse, if you prefer) is that brassieres are too hard to make for such small dolls, although Mattel makes swimsuit tops that could be copied, and if your doll *must* have a bra, I suggest you use the swimsuit top, or do as I have done and use a strip of lace to which straps are attached. The camisole is my answer to making a bra, and the fact that you can buy ready-made underpants made by Mattel is my excuse for not including a pattern for them here.

Let's define lingerie before we go any further. My *Oxford American Dictionary* defines lingerie only as women's underwear, but my *Synonym Finder* has two paragraphs of synonyms, which include nightclothes, robes, negligees, and peignoirs. I prefer to include all these garments in one chapter, since the only undies I have made patterns for are camisoles and half slips, both long and short.

The great bulk of the garments covered in this chapter are nightclothes: pajamas, nightgowns, robes, peignoirs, negligees, and bed jackets. They are all very fancy stuff, very feminine and pretty, and for the most part, easy to make if you follow directions carefully and consider the limitations of your fabric. If you have looked at the pictures and read the descriptions of materials used, you already know I didn't do much with really delicate fabrics.

Use Your Imagination!

Once again, as in every other chapter of this book, I will encourage you to use your own imagination to the fullest in trying out other combinations of fabric and color than what you see here.

Many of my ideas, especially those for the camisole, come from a catalog put out by a wonderful lingerie store in San Francisco, Victoria's Secret. My daughter Shannon suggested Victoria's Secret would be more appropriate for my purposes, because there is little emphasis on flagrantly sexy lingerie and more on beautifully made feminine things.

The Golden Dreams Barbie® Doll models a white nylon tricot camisole trimmed at top and bottom with two rows of scalloped lace. This is a very simple two-piece pattern shaped to fit the model without using darts.

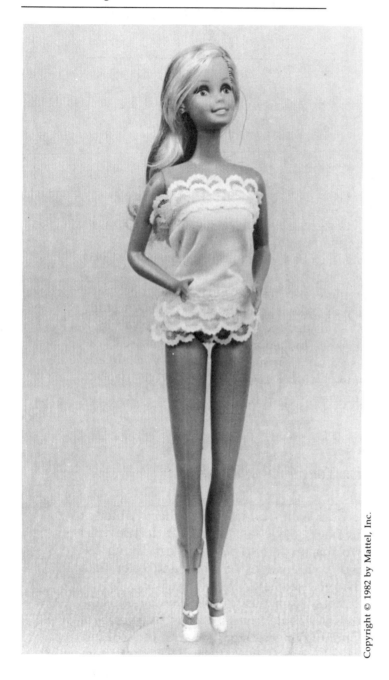

– – – – – – Seam

∿∿∿∿∿∿ Hem

THE CAMISOLE

The camisole is the most important of the undies shown here. You will note that the pattern is very simple, just two pieces, with the sides (waist) scooped out. You can add straps if you like. I have not because I don't want the straps to show in the event that the camisole is worn under a sheer blouse.

There are four examples of the camisole; a hot pink one and a pale pink one, a white one and a black one. The only differences among them are in the kinds of lace used for trim. They are all made from nylon tricot, for its stretchiness. Narrow in the middle and wide at top and bottom so they will slip over your doll's hips and fit snugly across breast and hips when pulled all the way up, they are very simple, almost fail-proof patterns.

I sew up one side, then add the lace to the top and bottom before sewing up the other side. You may notice on the hot pink one that there are little lace appliqués over the breasts in addition to the other trim. That was just a fanciful idea, inspired by the shape of the lace. The matching long slip has an appliqué on the front of the skirt, part of the same fanciful idea. They are both made from a very fancy, lacy slip I bought in a secondhand store just for this purpose.

PATTERN IX

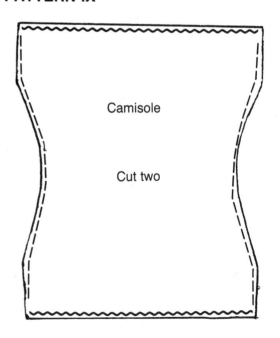

Camisole

Cut two

THE SLIP

The half slips are, as you see from the pattern, pieces of tricot in the shape of a rectangle, sewn up one side, top folded under one-quarter inch. A three-inch piece of elastic sewn over the fold on the wrong side (stretching the elastic as you sew) gathers the waist.

After the elastic is on, you should attach whatever lace or embroidery trim you like around the bottom of the slip before sewing up the other side. *Voilà*, a slip!

The only difference between a long slip and the short one is the length. I have used only tricot for slips because I had a lot of it, but, of course, you can use any other lightweight material. If you use satin, which is certainly a commonly used material for undies, I suggest you get lining satin, because it is lighter than standard satin and won't be so likely to wrinkle.

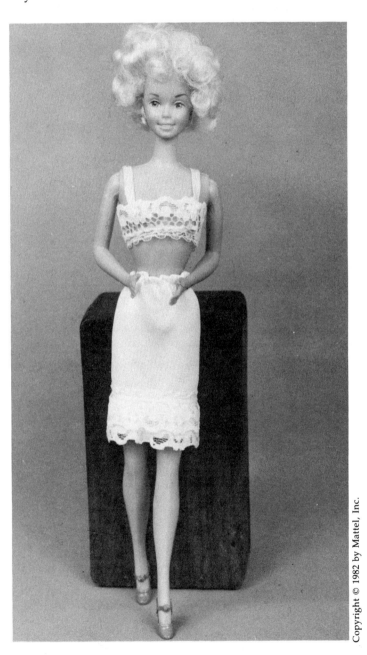

The Pretty Changes Barbie ® Doll models a cotton lace bra worn with a plain white tricot slip, which is trimmed with a synthetic lace that isn't quite as pretty as the cotton lace used in the bra. The bra takes about five minutes to make—no darts and no concern for exact fit. One might say this bra is just a modified camisole.

B

~~~~~~~~~ Hem

– – – – – – – Seam

Front Gathers

Slip

B

PATTERN X

Here is the same cotton lace bra worn by the Golden Dreams Barbie® Doll to complement her long half slip. The straps on this bra are made with narrow white satin ribbon and are measured exactly by pinning the strip of lace around the model's breasts, sticking the end of the ribbon under the lace in front, and bringing it over the shoulder, beyond the top of the lace in back. The strap is then cut and stitched into place. Very nice for a quick improvisation, isn't it?

The Parisian Barbie® Doll wears a black camisole over a same-fabric half slip. The camisoles shown are my answer to the problem of making brassieres for these tiny dolls. I have made brassieres and underpants, but they are such tiny little wisps and are so easily replaced by the bathing suits put out by Mattel, that I just gave up.

The Oriental Barbie® Doll sits on the old standby jewelry box, modeling the same pajamas worn by the Parisian Barbie® Doll in another picture. The difference between a blond model and a brunette model wearing exactly the same garment can be startling.

The other model is wearing the camisole, here made from a delicate pink nylon tricot, trimmed top and bottom with lace. Because of the stretch factor in this material and the shape of the pattern, it is simply two pieces sewn together along side seams. It slides readily over her legs and hips and fits perfectly over her bosom.

The Hispanic Barbie® Doll models a hot pink camisole over her long half slip of the same fabric. The material for these undies comes from a lady's slip bought in a thrift shop for one dollar, specifically to be used for lingerie for these tiny models. It is a very tightly knit, relatively heavy tricot, a gorgeous color, with delicate matching lace.

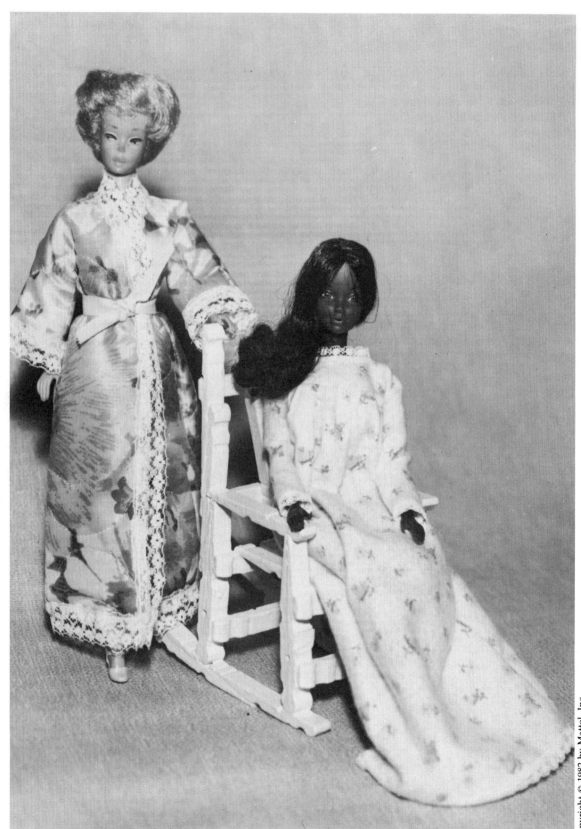

THE ROBE

You will see many examples of the bathrobe in quilted cotton and in quilted polyester fabric, as well as one in ice-blue velour. These are all made of the lightest-weight materials I could find. There isn't much choice in weights of polyester quilted fabric, and it is my opinion that most of those shown here would be prettier if they were less bulky. But we have to work with what is available.

The robes that aren't quilted would be better described as peignoirs or negligees, although they are all made from the same basic pattern, except for the one white-lace peignoir, which is made from a different pattern. I'm not crazy about that peignoir, so I made only one, but perhaps you can improve on that particular pattern.

Incidentally the robe pattern is exactly the same pattern as the one used for the long evening coat, so when you get to the long coats (Chapter Seven), just use the robe pattern. It might be a good idea to make two copies the first time, labeling one "robe" and the other "evening coat."

I have deviated from this basic pattern occasionally in order to make a garment less or more full, and I have sometimes cut it out as one single piece to avoid seams from the shoulders down the fronts of arms. There is, of course, no way to avoid an underarm seam, but the top seam can be eliminated and sometimes should be.

The way to cut this pattern as a single piece is to lay the back piece on your fabric, then match the front piece at the shoulder line, pin it down and cut the whole thing out as one piece. It is especially important to cut

down on the number of seams whenever you are using quilted or any other bulky material.

I have done this many times with the jacket pattern for the same reason. Seams add bulk to a finished garment, of course, and in general our purpose is to avoid bulk wherever possible.

The Oriental Barbie ® Doll models a plushy ice-blue velour robe here. The belt is not knotted because it is too bulky and would bunch up at the waist, but the ends *are* knotted, as a finishing touch.

The nightgown modeled by the Malibu Christie ® Doll, sitting in a rocking chair made from clothespins and spray painted, is concocted from very lightweight outing flannel used for baby clothes. A heavier flannel would not look as well on a sitting model. The standing Barbie ® Doll, modeling a flower-print quilted robe, is a very old doll, possibly manufactured as early as 1962. Note the nail polish on her fingernails. The two garments are trimmed with lace, and the robe has a grosgrain ribbon belt.

PATTERN XI

A Right Shoulder Seam

B Left Shoulder Seam

C Underarm-to-hem Seam

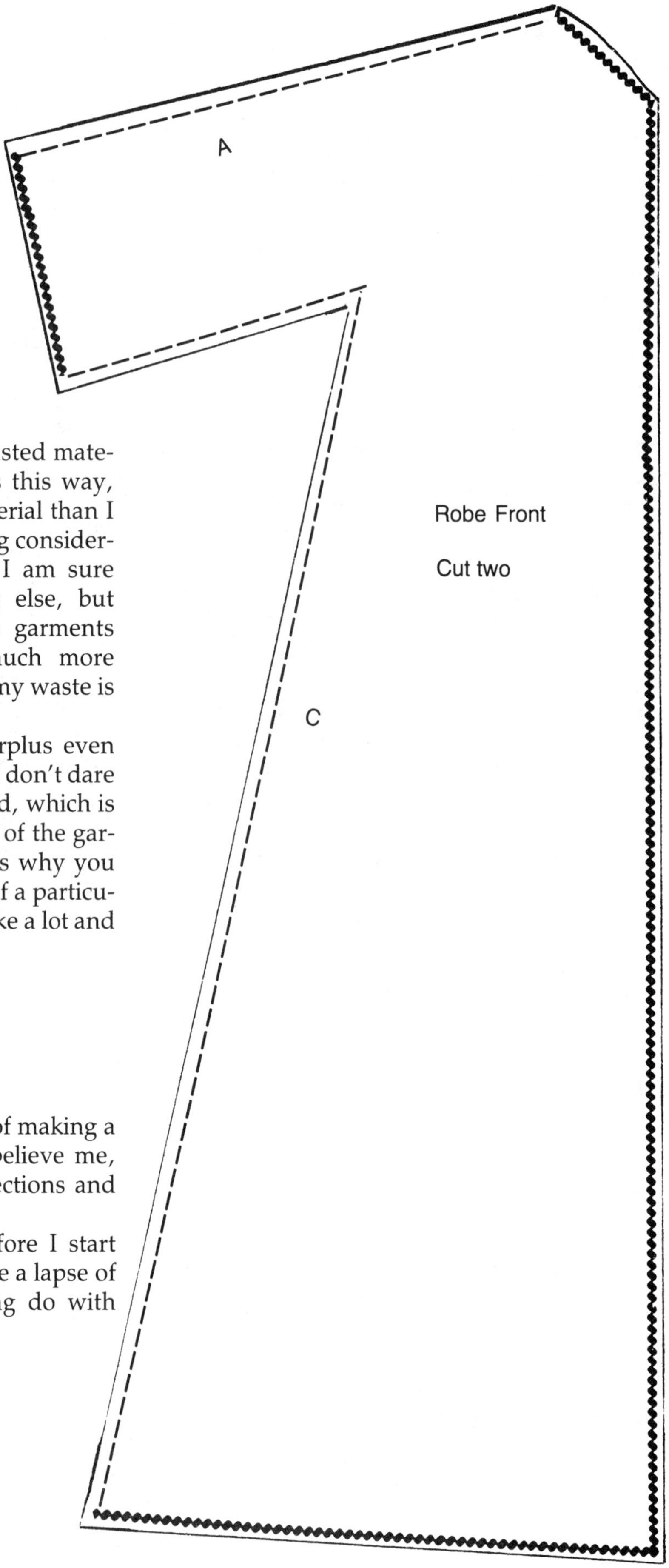

Wasted Fabric

There is always a little more wasted material when we cut out our patterns this way, but I usually have much more material than I can possibly use, so waste isn't a big consideration. I save all my scraps until I am sure I won't use them for something else, but because I use fabric from whole garments bought in secondhand stores much more often than I use brand-new fabric, my waste is excessive.

Actually, there is usually a surplus even when I buy new material, because I don't dare to ask for less than one-quarter yard, which is much more than we need for most of the garments in this book. It also explains why you see more than one garment made of a particular fabric: it's usually something I like a lot and can't bear to waste.

Getting It Together

Now for the simple mechanics of making a robe, peignoir, or negligee, and believe me, they *are* simple. If you follow directions and think ahead, you can't go wrong.

I always pick out my trim before I start cutting out a garment, unless I have a lapse of consciousness and end up making do with something that isn't exactly right.

A

Robe Front

Cut two

C

90

------- Seam
◆◆◆◆◆◆◆◆ Hem

B

Robe Back

Cut on fold

C

This gorgeous negligee, modeled by the Beauty Secrets Christie® Doll, was made from a very fancy half slip that had lots of lace around the hem. The lace had to be cut down to use on this small-scale garment, but it seems to have worked out very well.

The Malibu Christie® Doll shows yet another version of our basic bathrobe. This is a soft, cool, mint-green quilted polyester material that is easy to cut and sew. It does look a bit bulky on her, though, doesn't it? I really prefer a flatter cotton than these poufy quilted polyesters.

Three beautiful models pose in basic lingerie. The Barbie® Doll sitting on a small, carved, wooden box is wearing a quilted bed jacket made from blue-flowered cotton. Her pajama pants are white polyester, and her shoes are white clogs. Your First Barbie® Doll, on the left, wears a blue polyester quilted robe with a self-tie belt. Blue slides complete this outfit. The Golden Dreams Christie® Doll models a pajama set made of creamy off-white nylon tricot trimmed with slightly darker ecru cotton lace.

How Much Trim?

You should allow about one yard of lace, velvet or satin ribbon, or whatever you are using for robe trim. This amount includes all-around trim and enough for sleeve edging. If you look carefully at the negligees, you will see that I goofed on the white polyester one. The sleeves should have been trimmed; you can see the stitching, which would be completely hidden by the lace if it were there. Bad planning!

After you make this decision, your next step is to sew the pieces together across the shoulders, unless you have cut the robe out in one piece. Attach your sleeve trim before sewing up the sides from each sleeve edge and down the side all the way to the hem.

If you decide not to extend the trim around the bottom hemline, then you should take care of that hem now, whether you are sewing or fusing. I never hem anything that I plan to trim. I press the hem down and pin the trim to it, so I can attach trim and do the hemming in one step.

Any garment that has an unfinished look on the inside can be polished off very nicely by fusing lace over the unfinished edge, not using any more fusion tape than strictly necessary to avoid stiffening the fabric.

What Kind of Trim?

It should be fairly obvious to you that my favorite trim is lace, although you have probably taken note of the other trims I have used. I like velvet ribbon too, if my fabric is fairly stiff anyway, like the red quilted robe and the pajama outfit. Self-trim is often the best choice of all, as in the blue velour robe and the white robe with cornflower-blue sprigs. If you are going to use self-trim, you should always cut the strips on the bias rather than on the straight of the fabric, so that you are cutting across the straight all the way. Your trim strip will have more give if you cut it this way and will ravel less, although you should *always* allow for raveling when you cut narrow strips—don't cut them too narrow.

Good luck with your robe!

A white lace peignoir is modeled here by the Beauty Secrets Christie®. The fabric used for this robe is too stiff to look good with a belt.

The Italian Barbie® Doll wears another pair of pajamas, carefully cut from a half slip to preserve the white-on-white embroidery in symmetrical patterns for each leg of the pants.

Another pajama-robe combination here. The Parisian Barbie® Doll models a blue-flowered, quilted cotton robe. Her little wedgie-heel slides are an appropriate finishing touch. The blue chiffon pajamas, modeled by another old Barbie® Doll, demonstrate the versatility of this pattern. You can see through this fabric, and it is difficult to work with because it is so fragile, but the finished result is worth all the trouble.

The Beauty Secrets Christie® Doll models another bed jacket of blue quilted polyester fabric trimmed with lace and rounded off at the front corners to give a softer appearance than square corners. Her pajama pants are of a silky cotton mix with a tiny stripe woven in.

This gorgeous lounging robe is made from an actual robe for an adult woman. I wasn't sure the pattern would suit the Barbie® Doll scale, but it does because it is a very tiny print on the human scale. It is a silky finish fabric, probably rayon or nylon. The problem with using fabric from garments bought in secondhand stores or garage sales is that you often aren't able to establish exactly what the fabric is.

THE BED JACKET

The bed jacket is made exactly the same way the robe is, because it's the same pattern, only shortened. You can see from the pictures that the fabrics that work well for robes work equally well for bed jackets.

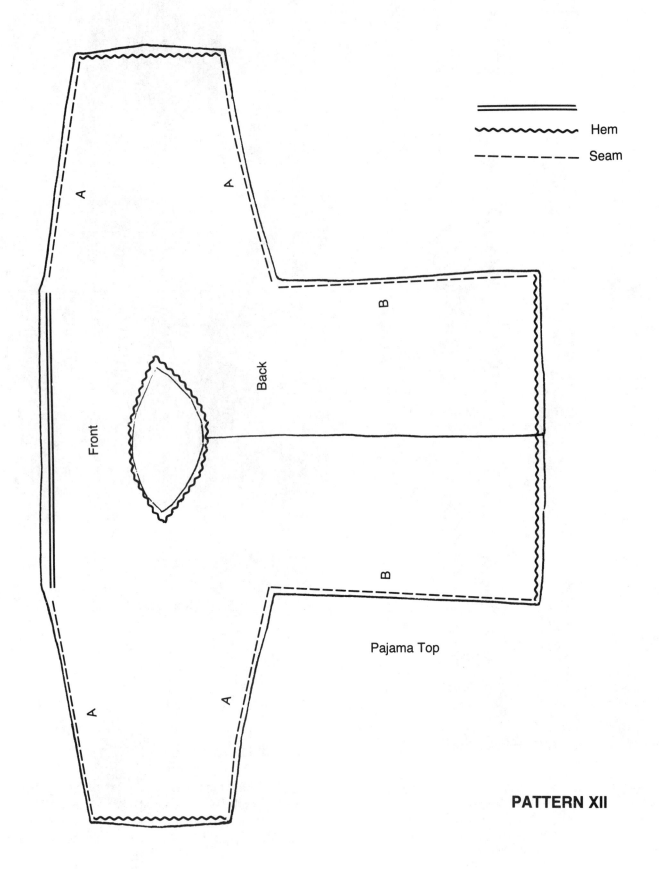

Hem

Seam

A

A

B

Front

Back

B

Pajama Top

A

A

PATTERN XII

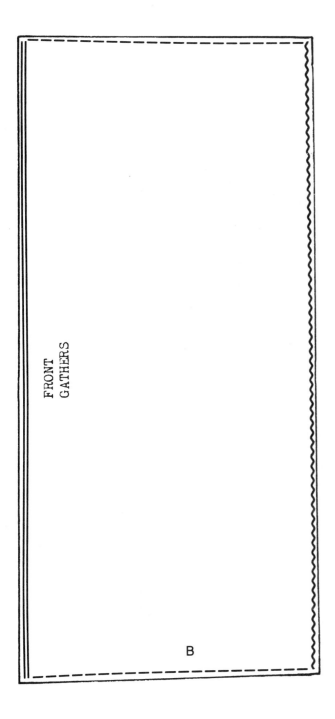

FRONT
GATHERS

B

PAJAMAS

This pattern is demonstrated in several different fabrics. The only thing all the fabrics have in common is that they are *lightweight*. The flannel is the lightest I could find, almost see-through when held up to the light or when compared to the sort of flannel used for kids' or adults' nightclothes.

My favorite of the five different pajamas shown is the white-on-white embroidered rayon. I had to cut this carefully to utilize the embroidered figure to the best advantage, but it came out very well, with a nice symmetry on matching legs and arms.

The hardest-to-make pair was the blue chiffon, because the material is so fragile it is very difficult to sew either by hand or by machine. I did all the edges by hand with teensy stitches, using a quilting needle and very fine silk thread. It is impossible to fuse this material, and almost impossible to use any sort of trim, because the weight of the gauziest lace would pull it out of shape.

The pajama pattern will probably look funny to you when you first see it, but think about the fold line representing the shoulder line, the longer half representing the back, and the small rectangular piece gathered and set into the front yoke, and you will get the picture. It's a little bit like a maternity smock, or even a bit like the smocked dresses toddlers wear, as you can see from the pictures. I made a lot of those little smocked dresses for my daughters when they were too young to talk back or sneer "sexist" at me because their brother got to wear flannel cowboy shirts that I also made. I thought I was inventing a new pattern when the idea for this came to me, but on second thought I realized the old yoked dress had been tucked away in my memory bank longer than I care to think about.

The pajama pants are made from the standard pants pattern, but I think harem pants would be terrific with this top, too. Both patterns are in Chapter Two.

The Beautiful Oriental Barbie® Doll leans against a miniature hamper, which is stuffed with quarters and nickels to make it heavy enough to support her weight balanced against it.

Don't you just love these quilted lounging pajamas? Quilted fabric usually has to be stitched over again to put the little squares into proper scale. I have done this with this particular cotton quilting to specially emphasize the tiny print. The jacket is trimmed with white velvet ribbon.

The Parisian Barbie® Doll poses in yet another version of the pajamas, made from the same outing flannel seen in the long granny nightgown.

The hamper should have been moved just a little bit closer to her chair, but the overall effect is charming, don't you agree?

This model wears a robe made from the wonderful quilted cotton fabric used for the lounging pajamas.

The robe is finished with a belt and piping of white velvet ribbon.

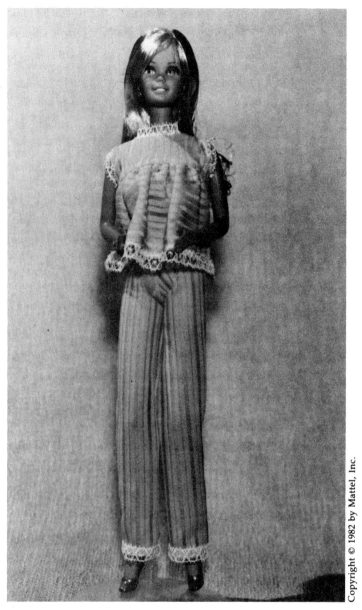

The Golden Dreams Christie® Doll looks comfortable in these polyester pajamas in a pale lavender shade, trimmed with tiny, narrow lace. Her nail polish-painted shoes carry off the color scheme.

THE NIGHTGOWN

The nightie is a very simple variation of the pajama pattern, which I just had to try out with the flannel. My kids make some very bad jokes about my granny nightgowns, but I still believe you can't beat a flannel nightie for cold winter nights.

This is the Ballet Barbie® Doll, with her hair just as it comes from the store. For fashion purposes her tutu had to come off. Isn't her hairdo stunning? And please note that she is still wearing her ballet slippers.

She is balanced against our miniature hamper here to show off her little quilted Chinese-style jacket over polyester pajama pants. I love the quilted fabric but had only a very small remnant.

The Golden Dreams Christie® Doll is shown here modeling a lace-trimmed bathrobe, the scale of which is a bit too large because I couldn't figure out how to double-quilt it without ruining the pattern. The belt is made from ribbon covered with the same lace.

FINAL NOTES

Review instructions before you start. Pick out your trim before cutting the pattern, and if you are using a self-trim, make sure you have enough fabric to cut the trim on the bias of the material before you cut out your individual pattern pieces.

And last of all, use your imagination!

The Ballet Barbie® Doll shows off a pair of lounging pajamas made from hot pink nylon tricot using the standard pants pattern and the jacket pattern. Both are cut a bit smaller because of the stretchability of this fabric, and because we want them to fit perfectly, not loosely. Charming, no?

This negligee, modeled by a blond Barbie® Doll, is made from a high-sheen polyester fabric with a slight silvery cast to it, trimmed with tiny matching lace, and finished off with a belt of the same fabric. The sleeves should have been trimmed with the lace, too, but it was too late when she arrived at the photographer's studio.

Chapter Five

The Evening Gowns

HERE ARE THREE evening gown patterns, each created for a specific purpose and a specific fabric.

The strapless dress is a classic by now: the dream of every sixteen-year-old girl contemplating her first prom and the despair of mothers who would like their daughters to maintain their (the moms') vision of virginal sweetness. I know because I've been there—on both ends. First I was the vestal virgin whose mother couldn't bear the thought of showing so much flesh at such a tender age, never mind the question of how the kid was going to keep the top of her dress from falling to her waist if she danced at all.

When my own daughters reached prom age, I tried to remember my outrage at my mother's gay nineties morality (I remembered snapping off those words at her), but all I could think about was how convulsed my girlfriends and I were at the prom when we compared notes on our mothers' reactions to our pleas for black strapless formals, and our collective disgust over the thought of a home-made dress.

My daughters both *chose* to make their own dresses, even after their father and I promised they could buy anything they wanted because we trusted their good taste, which had been developing a long time. They both made long slim sheath dresses with no sleeves and

long slits up the side for easy dancing. No flounces, no ruffles, and not a whole lot of bare flesh above the waist. They looked terrific.

You can see many versions of that strapless dress I wanted so badly to wear, and which I still believe is a perfect adornment for a great figure. I made the pattern for lamé fabric specifically, but as you can see, it works for almost everything. I only say almost because I haven't tried everything yet.

The circle skirt evening gown is shown in only one fabric, a sort of mock lamé that I just decided to do something different with. The tops are both adaptations of the basic blouse pattern used in so many of the daytime dresses. The strapless bodice must have a pleated or gathered skirt; it doesn't work well with a circle skirt.

The other basic evening gown, for which there is a one-piece pattern, is the off-the-shoulder, almost-straight sheath/toga. It is the easiest of the three to make, but there are some pitfalls the seamstress must adjust for. This dress works best with a stretchy fabric like Lurex or tricot. Because there are no darts, and indeed, no way to insert darts, the dress must fit well across your doll's bosom. We'll talk about possible problems with all three dresses later.

The Western Barbie® Doll shows off a beautiful dress with about twenty rows of creamy, crocheted lace. The only reason for such extravagance is that I bought about two hundred yards of this lace at a fire sale and can't imagine how I will ever find uses for it.

The dress is topped by a seal cape edged with fine black lace, which you can catch a glimpse of if you look closely at the neckline.

The Black Barbie® Doll demonstrates the ecru fringe dress without the matching shawl. This dress is made of drapery fringe sewn on in rows to a lightweight lining satin. It is made in two separate pieces, the bottom row on the bodice (row three) hangs over the waistband of the skirt. No point in attaching the two pieces, since they are easier to work with as separates.

The Black Barbie® Doll models a silver lamé dress topped by a rabbit fur coat, and her blond partner shows off a gold fabric dress with a circle skirt. They are leaning on a wooden jewelry box.

The Christie® Doll demonstrates this terrific dotted swiss evening dress with ruffles over the shoulders to simulate sleeves. She and her friend seem to be admiring the silver coffee service on the table covered with a red velvet holiday cloth. The Black Barbie® Doll models a silver lamé dress with rows and rows of brocade ruffles as she balances one of the coffee cups in her hands. Each of these dresses has seven shallow ruffles, discussed fully in Chapter Five.

The Parisian Barbie ® Doll poses in a blue Lurex dress topped by a dark-brown ranch mink stole. You can't see the top of this dress, but it is a simple strip crisscrossed in front and sewn to the waistband of the skirt. I have not included the pattern because this dress always ruins the doll's hairdo if pulled over her head. The only alternative is to take the head off before slipping the loop around the model's neck.

This model is balanced against our old standby jewelry box prop to show her velvet jacket and heavily ruffled skirt to best advantage. I originally intended to make a plain blouse top for this dress by sewing rows of the lace together flat and cutting the pattern from it, but then I tried this little velvet jacket on over the skirt and decided not to bother with a top.

Your First Barbie® Doll models another beautiful lace gown, this one embellished with two rows of seed pearls and sequins. The scallops that edge this lace are about one inch across, a perfect scale for a skirt that measures eight inches around and is tightly pleated at the waistline to make it stand out. It is lined with a fairly stiff white polyester to give it body.

Her fur coat is very dark brown rabbit fur, and is not lined because it is already very bulky. The fur is particularly dense.

A lovely combination, don't you agree?

The Golden Dreams Barbie® Doll displays a classic toga/sheath dress. This sensational dress is made from black Lurex with diagonal rows of silver thread woven in. Cutting this fabric on the bias is the way to make the pattern diagonal rather than straight. It is bound on all edges with a narrow strip of silver lamé, including the waistline to create the illusion of a separate bodice. This is actually a single-piece pattern.

Choosing Fabrics

If you have looked over the pictures of evening gowns, you know that I will go to great lengths for variety. You have seen everything from plain old cotton through velvet, lace, nylon, dotted swiss, Lurex, brocade, and finally, several colors of lamé. Before we go any further, let me tell you again that the way to pronounce lamé is *lah-may*, and the way to pronounce tricot is *tree-co*.

My needlecraft book defines lamé as a shimmery metallic cloth, usually a crepe weave. That doesn't tell us much, does it? What we really need to know about *any* fabric is how to use it, what kind of needle, what kind of thread, what about cutting across the grain, whether it requires a hot iron or a cool one.

To answer those questions in order: (1) a ballpoint needle, if you're sewing by machine, (2) medium-weight thread, (3) cutting across the grain of lamé is fine, but there is no point in cutting on the bias, (4) *never* iron lamé on the right side, and *always* use a cool iron on any metallic material. Better yet, use a press cloth. In my opinion the only way to hem metallic fabric is by using iron-on fusion tape.

Lamé is expensive and it is sometimes hard to find. Most big yardage stores stock it during the holidays, but they may not have it in the middle of summer, so it's a good idea to telephone first if you are in doubt.

I have never seen lamé on sale, and I've never bought it secondhand because I have not seen any that was in good enough condition to use again. It gets a tarnished look when it is old.

I have paid as low as $8.99 a yard and as high as $12.99 a yard, which may be just normal inflation. It is sometimes as wide as sixty inches, which means that you can get several garments from just one-quarter yard (nine inches). This is deep enough for you to cut long skirts off both selvage ends if you don't mind cutting across the straight grain. I don't think it matters how you cut lamé; the matte finish on the metallic side looks the same either way.

All the other metallic fabrics you see in the formal-wear pictures are secondhand. The gold brocade coat worn by the Oriental Barbie® Doll comes from a terrible-looking blouse with very full sleeves. It was one of the ugliest garments I ever saw, but the fabric was just divine for this coat. You can't see the lining from the picture, so you might assume this fabric is more substantial than it really is. It actually has the same filmy look and feel as fine chiffon and would have been an absolute horror to sew if I hadn't lined it first. I used a wine-colored rayon lining, because the main color in the fabric was a deep dark red. The gold pattern in the material sort of shimmers against that maroon lining.

The silver brocade coat, shown earlier, worn by the Oriental Barbie® Doll comes from another hopelessly ugly secondhand garment, an evening skirt fit only for the Witch of Endore. It is, as you can probably tell from the picture, very stiff, unyielding material, perfect for making a long coat with a stand-up collar, but totally useless for making dresses. I tried to make bodices from it, but was ready to blow my brains out after two tries.

The red dresses with gold borders, worn by the Parisian Barbie® and the Hispanic Barbie® Dolls are perfect examples of a very productive shopping binge in a secondhand store. The original garment was a cocktail dress, fully lined, with a wide gathered skirt. The gold border ran all around the hem of the skirt, as well as on the sleeves and around the neckline. I have a couple of yards of it still stashed away.

Other Options

Your choices are limited only by your imagination and your pocketbook. I have used curtain fabric that turned into gorgeous dresses; old tablecloths of lace should never be thrown out if you make doll clothes—at least not without a good careful check for usefulness as fabric first.

Lace is a particular favorite of mine. Although all lace has a certain degree of fragility just because of its openness, and must generally be attached to an underskirt, if only to give a semblance of body, it is very easy to work with once you get the hang of it and figure out what works and what doesn't.

The black lace dress worn by the Hispanic Barbie® Doll is a case in point of what works. I bought the lace for this dress at a garage sale for fifty cents; it was a single strip about 1½ yards long. I thought the scallops might be too big, but for fifty cents, how could I lose?

The first thing I determined when I got home was that the scallops were just perfect for a bodice, if I put a very tiny dart in on each side, straight up—well, almost straight, because the dart tapers to a point. It looked like a sweetheart line, a valentine dress. I cut off enough for the bodice, then simply folded the remaining lace twice so I could tell how much fabric I had left for each of four deep ruffles. Then I pleated each ruffle lightly, made a narrow underskirt (5 inches wide and 7 inches long) to which I sewed the ruffles in descending rows.

Always start at the hemline when sewing ruffles to an underskirt, so you are able to control the evenness of the overhang from the next ruffle and attach it in a perfectly straight line. That sounds like something any amateur would do as a matter of course, but if you are using slippery fabric for the underskirt, it can be a problem, and if a ruffled skirt isn't perfectly aligned, if it looks the tiniest bit awry, you will be disappointed. All it takes is one crooked ruffle to spoil a dress.

It took less than an hour to make this dress from absolute scratch, and I figure it couldn't have cost me more than seventy-five cents total, and probably less since the underskirt was just a scrap of lining fabric, and how much thread could it take? Maybe a nickel's worth?

The other ruffled-skirt dresses have many more rows, all except the red and gold one. I call it the Flamenco for obvious reasons. Can't you just imagine this beautiful Spanish doll twirling and tapping out a flamenco rhythm with her heels?

But to get back to the many-ruffle dresses, let's talk about the white dotted swiss and the silver lamé with brocade ruffles. They both have fitted hip skirts, that is, the ruffles don't begin at the waist, but are dropped to mid-hipline, as in the Flamenco.

I hope it won't shock you to be told that the dotted swiss is plain old curtain fabric, very sheer, so the bodice is completely lined. To make the self-ruffles for this dress, I cut several long strips of fabric 1⅛-inches wide. I fused the hems on all the strips before ruffling, and since I didn't have a ruffle attachment for my old machine, I simply pleated the strips, using a toothpick to push the pleats into place as I stitched. The little over-the-shoulder pieces are leftover ruffling. The decision to use them as such was a last-minute shot in the dark, but I like the different look they impart to the entire garment. How about calling this dress Sweet Sixteen?

The silver brocade ruffles on the other dress are not nearly as full, because the brocade is very stiff and would have stood straight out if they had been much fuller. I attached these ruffles and the ones on the dotted swiss from the top down, because the first ruffle had to be topstitched. It's a bit harder to keep the lines of ruffles straight when they're put on this way, but as always, the result justifies the special effort, doesn't it?

The white cotton lace ruffled dress shown with a velvet jacket is another story altogether. I gathered (pleated, actually) about ten yards of this lace, knowing I wanted many rows of ruffles. I also knew I needed to use some of it up since there are about two hundred yards left on the spool. I wasn't sure how many rows it would take, but since I didn't care how much I used, I didn't bother to measure in advance. It turned out to be fourteen rows—not the most terrific ruffled dress I've ever made, but worth showing if only to demonstrate the finished product. In contrast to the black lace dress, which took about one hour total to make, this one took me about three hours of endlessly sewing on row after row of lace.

Lamé bell-shape skirts are, without exception in these pictures, nine inches wide. They could be narrower, but anything wider tends to bunch up if you want to sit your doll down. Check the pictures and you will see one of a blond Barbie® Doll sitting on the black piano bench as her black friend stands to the side of the piano. The blonde is wearing a white brocade skirt topped with lamé, and you can see how the skirt bunches up as she sits. It is actually no more full than the teal-blue skirt of the

The Hispanic Barbie® Doll, looking especially beautiful here, models a stunning evening gown made entirely from lace that I bought for fifty cents in a thrift shop in San Francisco. Obviously a leftover piece from something made for a real live person, it was about two feet long and about two inches wide, just about enough for this dress.

Her necklace is made from an earring hung on a heavy black thread.

The Golden Dreams Christie® Doll, standing next to the baby grand piano, looks ready to clap her hands, as well she might when modeling this stunning teal-blue lamé evening dress trimmed with cotton braid.

Her blond modeling partner, posing in a dress made from the same pattern, this time of a heavy white brocade shot through with silver threads, smiles back. The bodice and hem of her dress are trimmed with silver braid bought in a dime store.

The Ballet Barbie® Doll's loose-flowing hair adds something special to her pose in this wonderful dress, which is made from a tricot half slip with a small lace insert at the hem. The tricot is very shiny, like taffeta, and quite stiff for a doll dress. The bodice is made from rows of sequins sewn to elastic material and requires no darts because it stretches across the Barbie® Doll's breasts. It is attached to the skirt by means of a black satin ribbon waistband.

Isn't she a knockout?

The Parisian Barbie® Doll poses serenely on the wicker settee to show to best advantage her classic strapless evening gown, in this case made from pure cotton. Because the skirt fabric is very lightweight and quite sheer, it is cut a full two inches wider than the standard nine-inch skirt pattern. Both bodice and skirt are fully lined.

Note her rhinestone choker, which is fastened with a piece of thread in back. Making jewelry for these tiny models is almost as much fun as making their clothes.

These two dresses are my crowning achievement. My editor suggested in a joking way that I might figure out how to make a high-fashion hula-skirt for the Hawaiian Barbie® Doll. I took him literally, and this is the happy result.

Hardly a high-fashion hula dress, this is made by sewing rows of drapery fringe, carefully overlapped, to flat pieces of material of the same color. Both dresses have single-row fringe shawls which are draped differently to give the two effects. The Italian Barbie® Doll's shawl is draped from front to back to create the illusion of a V-neckline. The Ballet Barbie® Doll's shawl is draped loosely over her shoulders to hang down in front and expose the top of the bodice. How do you like her headband?

other doll, but because of the heaviness of the brocade it still bunches. I don't know what the answer is except not to use such heavy, stiff fabric in the first place. I have tried to make a circle skirt from this stuff, but the result is just ridiculous.

Softer fabrics can be fuller, of course, as you can see from the cotton flowered skirt/hot pink bodice on the Parisian Barbie® Doll. This skirt is a bit over eleven inches wide—so wide it looks like a hoop skirt, though it has only a little narrow slip underneath. Beautiful, isn't it? Really shows the effectiveness of cotton fabric when used to the best advantage.

There are just three more dresses I want to mention before we get on with instructions on how to sew them all.

The black dress with the lace insert in the skirt is made from the bottom edge of a woman's half slip. I bought that slip especially for the insert, which happened to be the smallest lace insert I've ever seen; just exactly right for a dress like this one. The fabric is a rather heavy tricot, which looks almost like taffeta here, don't you agree? The bodice for this dress comes from strips of sequins sewn to a sort of loose elastic backing. The strip was a little narrow for my purposes, so I added a black ribbon waistband before attaching it to the skirt. Another case of a quick improvisation to achieve a particular result.

I want to tell you about the two dresses made from drapery fringe now, because they are among the easiest-to-make dresses in this section.

My editor, after being told there was a Hawaiian Barbie® Doll, suggested I think about a high-fashion hula skirt, which immediately raised the image in my mind of twenties flapper dresses with rows and rows of fringe. I'm sure it was said in jest, but I just had to follow through on my little image. This is drapery fringe, bought in the upholstery and drapery department of one of the largest yardage stores in San Francisco. The cost is about $1.50 a yard and these dresses take about three yards. It is cut in five-inch strips and sewn to a straight piece of matching lining material. The top and skirt are not sewn together because the bottom row of fringe on the bodice overhangs the top row on the skirt. It's hard to count the exact number of rows in these pictures because of the draped fringe over both dolls' shoulders, but I believe there are ten rows on each dress; three on the bodice and seven on the skirt. You can see that the drapes are different; the black one is draped from the front and pulled down to form a sort of V-line, while the cream-colored one is draped from the back to hang down from the doll's shoulders and to show the line at the top of the bodice. I tried headbands with both dresses, and ended up using only one because the other one didn't really show up and the contrasting looks of the two together seemed important.

Next, let's have a few words about the sheath/toga dresses. You have seen three examples of this dress, two of which are somewhat hidden by the maribou boa draped around the dolls' shoulders. The third one, worn by the Hispanic Barbie® Doll, is made of a rather stiff, teal-blue Lurex, which is just perfect for this dress, since it is okay for it to hang straight and even look a little bit stiff.

Of the two covered up by boas, there is a soft blue Lurex on the Black Barbie® Doll, and you can see that this soft fabric doesn't bunch up around her hips when she sits. The other blue one, made of a synthetic that has the look of permanent accordion pleats, is my favorite, but there is an obvious flaw in this dress. I cut it from the bottom (hemline) of a dress so that I wouldn't have to hem it myself, but I'm not crazy about the machine hem that shows. Now I wish I had covered that hemline with a small row of lace. The best thing about this dress is the neat way it hangs and sort of hugs the doll's figure at the hipline.

Instructions for Cutting and Sewing

First, the basic strapless evening gown, which is made from a two-piece pattern. For lamé I cut a rectangle nine inches wide by seven inches deep, but I cut the skirt wider for more flexible fabrics. If there are selvages on my fabric, I always use the selvage for the bottom of my skirt, because it fuses easily.

If you measure your doll from waist to floor, you will see that seven inches is exactly right for length of skirt, with room for a one-

This lovely blond model shows her off-the-shoulder blue accordion-pleated dress to good advantage. The boa is made from trimmed maribou, which is too long for these little dolls so it must be trimmed. As you can see, it fluffs right up after being cut with ordinary scissors.

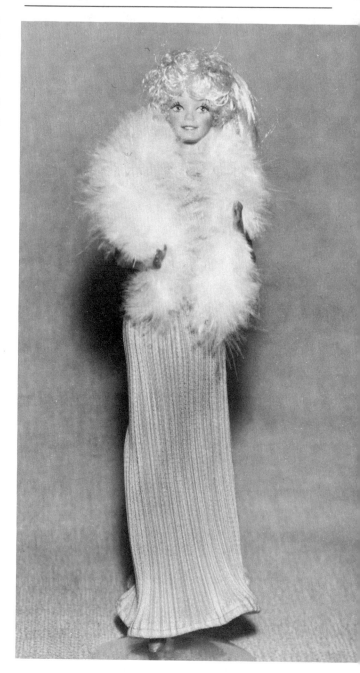

Two lovely ladies at the piano. The Malibu Barbie® Doll shows off her black and gold brocade coat over a matching dress, while Black Barbie displays a blue and silver Lurex toga/sheath dress. Her softly draped, old-fashioned maribou boa barely shows the line of this off-the-shoulder gown.

The Hispanic Barbie® Doll models an off-the-shoulder toga/sheath in teal-blue and silver Lurex. Unlike the other togas, this is made from very stiff fabric, which helps to hold the severe line. Toga gowns are easily made from a single-piece pattern.

The Hispanic Barbie® Doll models a standard evening dress made of hot pink satin for the bodice and deep purple velvet for the skirt. Her little stole is constructed from border lace and is simply decorative, rather than useful as protection from the cold.

Her partner shows the same dress made in a different combination of fabrics. This brocade top, which looks like tapestry, comes from a piece of flat hemmed material that I bought at a thrift shop in Berkeley, California. I was never able to figure out what it had been used for, unless it was to cover a small table, like a runner. Her skirt is black velvet.

B-17. The Beauty Secrets Barbie® Doll models a watermelon red lamé dress with a jewel-tone tapestry bodice. Her honey-colored mink cape is a lovely finishing touch for this terrific dress.

quarter-inch hem. It is more difficult to measure your doll from waist to top of bosom, but I assure you the bodice measurement will work.

THE BODICE

Cut a rectangle 4½ inches by 2½ inches. Mark your darts on the wrong side of the fabric, then fuse the top and side edges to no more than ¼ inch. I use only the up-and-down darts for most fabrics, but you will have to make that decision for yourself. I find that using all four darts is important only for certain woven fabrics, like tapestry material, in order to shape the bodice perfectly.

THE SKIRT

After determining the width skirt you need, you will fuse the skirt hem, then gather or pleat it at the waist to measure 3½ inches when finished. I always turn under the edges of the skirt where the waist meets in back before I start pleating. I always pleat because I think the material is distributed more evenly than when gathered, and in general, pleating is just a better way to control fabric.

Then I lay the bodice on the skirt, bottom edge of bodice to waist edge of skirt, right sides together. I sew them together along the line of stitching that holds the pleats in place, taking particular care to make sure of covering it.

The very last operations are to sew up the back of the skirt and to add a snap at the waistline in back. If something has gone wrong (and lots has for me) and the closure is tight, you can use a hook-and-eye closure to give you that tiny bit of extra room.

Let me just tell you that I had to fool around with bodices for quite a while to get them exactly right. So much depends on how much stretch and give there is in your fabric with these very exacting measurements. Another good idea is to do the darts first of all, and then fuse the edges, because if the darts are a tiny bit off center, you can compensate by the amount of fabric you turn under at the edges.

In any case, I advise you to make a couple of trial runs. Test your fabric for stretch, put in the darts, and try it on the doll to see how well it works.

PATTERN XIII

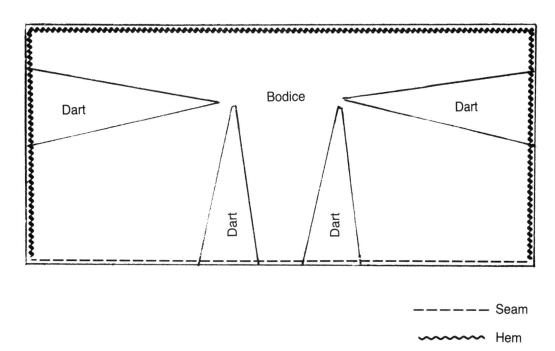

Dart

Bodice

Dart

Dart

Dart

– – – – – – Seam

〰〰〰 Hem

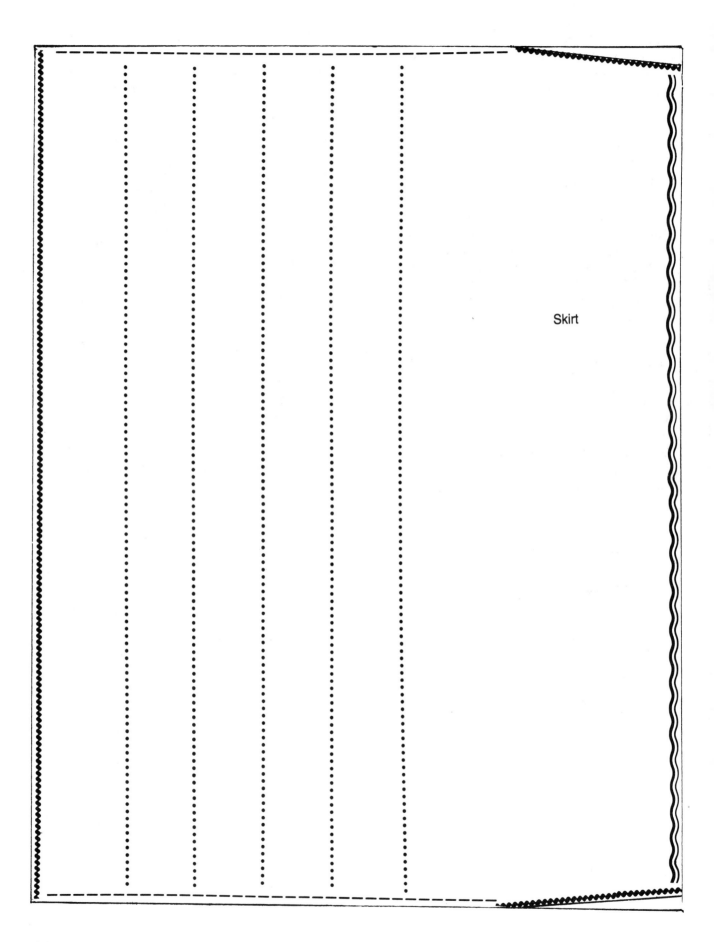

Skirt

PATTERN XIV

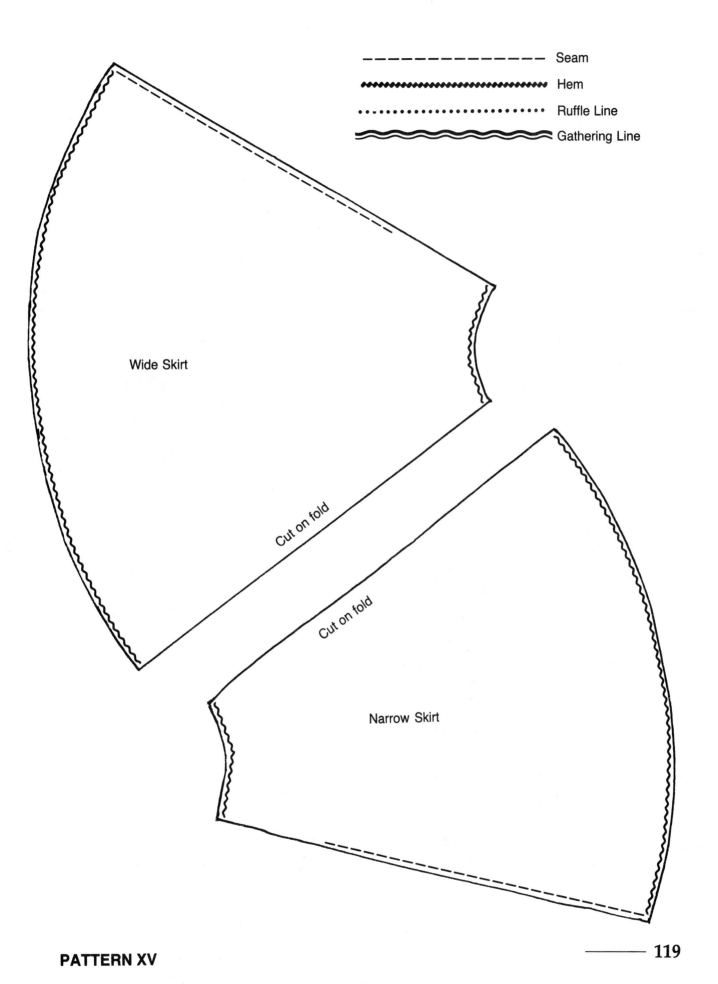

Seam

Hem

Ruffle Line

Gathering Line

Wide Skirt

Cut on fold

Cut on fold

Narrow Skirt

PATTERN XV

119

The Parisian Barbie® and the Hispanic Barbie® Dolls model two very different dresses made from the same basic pattern and from exactly the same fabric, a stiff border print.

The dress on the left is obviously our basic evening gown, but it should be noted that this particular material has to be cut very carefully to get the maximum benefit of the gold border.

The ruffled skirt on the right is made with only four ruffles, unlike any of the other ruffled dresses shown so far. These are relatively deep ruffles, and the reason for using such depth is that this is very difficult material to work with because it is so stiff.

The Oriental Barbie® Doll steps forward to balance her hip against the piano so she can pose without a stand. Her modeling partner, the Black Barbie® Doll, sits on the piano stool to show her dress to best advantage.

The dress on the left is gold lamé with a gold Lurex top, over which she wears a brocade coat trimmed with the same lamé to point up the gold threads in her coat. This particular brocade is very fine see-through material, which had to be lined to give it substance.

The dress modeled by the Black Barbie® Doll is made of the same fabric you have already seen in another similar dress. I don't know quite what to call this fabric, but I do know it is not standard lamé, unless it is very old and has softened with age. It doesn't have the stiffness associated with new lamé.

THE CIRCLE SKIRT

This one is easy and fast, since there is no pleating or gathering. You can see from the examples pictured that I have made a seam straight down the front of this skirt.

Of course, you can cut this skirt out in one piece if you have enough fabric; the only reason I didn't was that my fabric wasn't wide enough. I had only a long narrow strip, so instead of cutting on a fold, I just doubled the material and cut two. The choice of a front seam was made to avoid the possibility of spoiling the line with side seams, in which case I would have had to make a placket for the back closure. If the fabric had been too narrow to even get two pieces this size, I'd have made an eight-gore skirt. We haven't done anything with gored skirts in this book, though I was tempted more than once, just because one sees them everywhere. If there is a later revision of this book, I will probably use the revised edition for an excuse to do some of the things I didn't have time for in this one. And I certainly urge you to give it a whirl (sorry, no pun intended) if you have smaller pieces that you desperately want to use.

The way to do it is to fold your pattern into quarters—remember the pattern is only for half a skirt and must be cut out on folded fabric, one edge against the fold. So, one-quarter of this pattern equals one-eighth of a complete skirt. You must allow for eight seams, so after you have drawn a quarter piece on paper, you must add one-quarter inch on either side for a seam allowance, then cut out eight pieces and sew them together, one by one. Press each seam flat before hemming or fusing. You can see that mine are fused, since no stitches are visible.

Fusing a circle skirt is a little tricky, but you will get the knack if you press the hem into place before inserting the fusion tape and pressing the two sides together.

The Parisian Barbie® Doll poses in a very full-skirted dress, showing the pretty flowered print. The solid color bodice is completely covered by her luxurious short mink coat. This is called Tourmaline mink. She is a lovely model, isn't she?

121

THE BODICE

The most important point I want to make about this dress is that it is an improvisation to utilize the maximum amount of this fabric, which as I have mentioned already was in one long strip.

The bodices are adaptations of the basic blouse pattern (without the sleeves) on page 63. You can see that I have topstitched the fronts of both bodices and that I have made plunging necklines on both of them, which are fused in the same way the skirt hems are.

Use your imagination. Improvise! Try anything once, and who knows what you might come up with? Perhaps a totally new design.

THE TOGA/SHEATH DRESS

This is a single-piece pattern, which you must cut on the fold of the material. The seam is on the short side of the pattern, so that the longer side can have a small swoop, undisturbed by a seam.

After sewing up the side, you must hem or fuse all the top edges. I have opted for fusing for the same old reason: to avoid the sight of stitching along edges.

Be careful not to cut the armhole too deep; this is the only tricky part of this dress. And when you fuse (or hem) this armhole, press it down first and try it on your doll before actually finishing it.

The three examples you see are just sewn together at the shoulder line, but it is possible to finish it differently, if you want to take the trouble to extend the neck and armhole lines, cutting a long narrow strip that could be used to tie the dress at the shoulder. I have made a few like that but am never satisfied with finishing the edges and then tying it. The finished edge makes it too bulky for a nice soft bow at the shoulder. Another option would be to attach ribbon of the same color and to use the ribbon for a tie.

This is the old standby toga/sheath dress of blue Lurex shot through with silver threads. It drapes nicely from shoulder to floor on this Black Barbie® Doll. Too bad her shoulder line isn't as softly rounded as some of the other models, but she is a perfectly stunning model when her shoulders are covered.

The little bangle bracelets of bamboo are contrived from basket links.

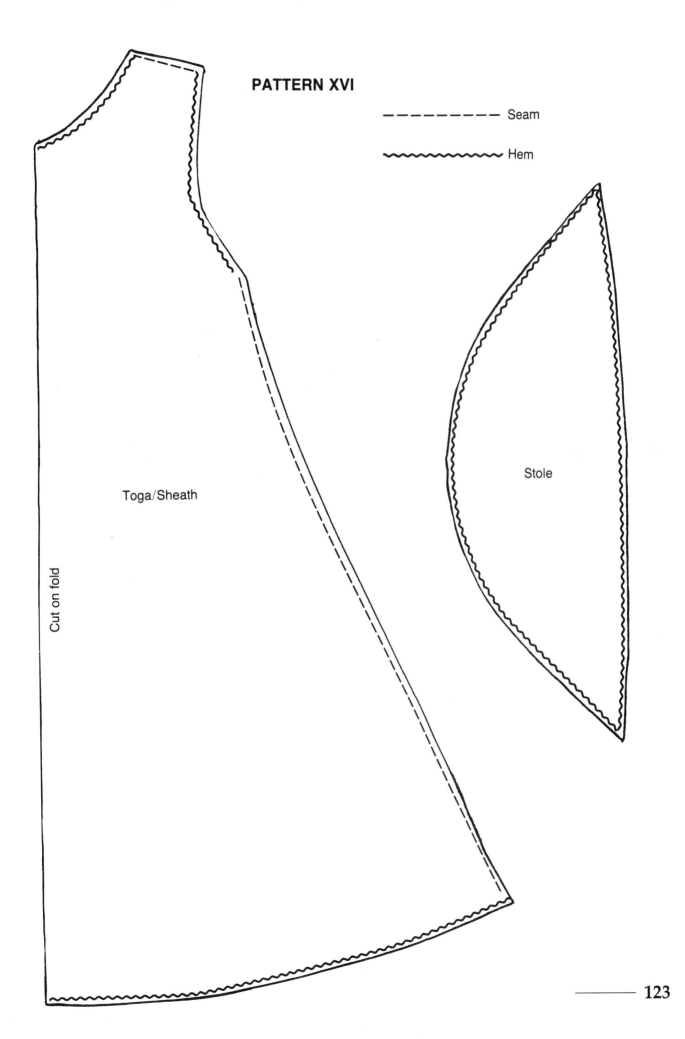

PATTERN XVI

– – – – – Seam

∿∿∿∿∿ Hem

Toga/Sheath

Cut on fold

Stole

This model poses in a deep mauve lamé dress, beautifully complemented here by a soft white bunny fur stole. The standing urn, filled with plastic lilies of the valley, completes this pretty scene.

The Western Barbie Doll's cuddly rabbit fur coat almost covers her beautiful, sheer, scarf-print dress. Because this neon pink and orange fabric is so sheer, there are two layers in the skirt as well as a long half slip underneath. The bodice, which you can't see, is completely lined.

How do you like her matching hat?

The Golden Dreams Barbie® Doll sitting pretty on the piano stool, with her legs stretched out to show the fullness in the legs of this evening jumpsuit, demonstrates the versatility of the blue/silver Lurex once again. Her shawl of fine sheer chiffon, trimmed with a flocked design, was bought expressly for the purpose seen here.

The Beauty Secrets Christie ® Doll wears a deep mauve lamé dress trimmed with cotton braid on the bodice. Her gorgeous honey-colored mink coat points up the soft sheen of the lamé.

The Hispanic Barbie ® Doll models a fake-fur coat trimmed with bunny fur. Isn't she darling in this stark black-and-white costume?

The Golden Dreams Barbie® Doll waves to the audience. Her backswept hair makes it possible for us to see the full glory of her coat, which is a reddish-brown rabbit fur. The frosty pink satin dress with a hot pink satin bodice completes this gorgeous pose.

We haven't been able to identify this doll, even with the aid of the *Collectors' Barbie® Doll Encyclopedia*. She has thick straight red hair and a pronounced tan. I believe her to be at least ten years old—perhaps older. She models a shimmery gold lamé-like dress here, topped by a rich-brown ranch mink stole.

The upswept hairdo worn by the Italian Barbie®
Doll adds to the glamour of her silver lamé and Lurex
dress, which is topped by a simple wool shawl bor-
dered with dime store braid.

I am especially fond of this particular model because of her fine Roman face. She is endowed with a
beautiful straight nose.

It Ain't Easy!

Just a few last-minute things to remember before you start making any of these beautiful evening gowns.

First, keep in mind the fact that if you make a mistake, before you get angry or discouraged, put it down, go have a cup of tea and look calmly out the window (if you have a pretty view), and tell yourself that if there's a way to salvage it, you can find that way. Don't just toss it out and start over, unless you can afford to waste fabric.

Second, save any scraps that are big enough to practice fusing on. There *is* an art to fusing two sides of fabric together, but the only way I have found to get it together is practice, practice, and more practice. If you get the fusing material on your iron, turn the heat up and with heavy strokes of the iron on cotton, wipe it off. You'll ruin the cotton, but you'll have a clean iron to start over with.

My last caution is simple. Until you have made a few of these dresses, pin them to your doll before attaching bodices to skirts. There is so little margin for error when using such tiny pieces that you just have to take every possible precaution to avoid error. I have made so many of these dresses I can almost tell by looking at the pieces of a dress ready to be put together whether there is going to be a problem. But I still put the bodice on the doll, pin the skirt on over the bottom of the bodice, and stand back to look at it from all angles before doing the final act of attaching the two pieces.

And now let me wish you success and satisfaction. May you have the best-dressed doll in town!

Here's another look at the Italian Barbie® Doll showing off a cool summery fringe dress. Her stole of the same fringe is draped from front to back to create the effect of a V-neckline. This is one of my favorite dresses of the collection, elegant while at the same time simple. It is also very easy to make.

Chapter Six

Fur and Leather

W E WILL DEAL with fur and leather in this chapter because they have several common properties. Both require the use of leather needles because the sharp-wedge point goes through them. Fur, of course, has a leather backing.

The soft suedes and glove leathers I use don't require much different treatment than ordinary fabric, aside from the importance of using a special needle and remembering never to pin any kind of leather because the pinholes won't close up when the pin is withdrawn.

Fur

Let's deal with fur first, since it is different from anything else we have discussed so far. The coat pattern was arrived at after more trials and tribulations than you would care to contemplate, so I won't bore you with them, but will just give you the benefit of my experience.

Fur must be cut with a knife, either a special leather knife, which you can buy from a furrier or a leather shop, or a plain old X-Acto knife. You will need plenty of blades in either case because leather very quickly dulls even the sharpest blade.

I used embroidery scissors to cut the leather in the very first fur coat I made for the Barbie ® Doll, and it wasn't a complete disaster only because I carefully guided the scissors through the fur. When the coat came out well, I decided to find out if I could buy fur scraps from a furrier I knew, who enlightened me on several scores. He asked if I needed a leather knife and when I asked, "What for?", he asked how I'd been cutting my fur. He laughed his head off when I told him, then showed me the right way and sold me a proper leather cutter. I have since abandoned that particular cutter because it is very hard to change blades, and the X-Acto knife does just as good a job. Changing blades is much easier on the X-Acto, and I like the feel of holding a knife with a proper handle.

I also found out that day that buying fur scraps from a furrier is very expensive, because the pieces are never big enough for a full coat, and if they were, they would cost more than the finished coat could possibly sell for. I have since then also abandoned the notion of making fur coats to sell, after figuring out I was working for about fifty cents an hour to sell the coats for a price anyone would pay. But they are a lot of fun to make for special gifts or for a Barbie ® Doll fashion show, so I still make them.

This lovely model poses in a chinchilla fur coat worn with a pair of vinyl pants. Her right leg is braced against a carved wooden jewelry box so she can stand unassisted. We have not been able to identify this doll, even with the aid of our encyclopedia, but isn't she stunning? Note the topstitching on her pants, which were cut out in such a way as to preserve the stitching on the garment they are made from.

What Kind of Fur?

I am partial to mink and chinchilla. Of course! Who wouldn't be, you may ask yourself.

But the reason for my partiality isn't what you think. Forget the fact that they are two of the most expensive furs around, and certainly two of the lushest and most beautiful. Just forget that for the moment.

The *real* reason is that they are both short-hair furs, in comparison to just about anything else you might mention. I have made lots of rabbit fur coats, because rabbit is easier to find in secondhand stores and much less expensive, but I won't buy it if it's really long. It's too hard to work with in such small pieces, and it doesn't even look good on the doll when it is finished, if the fur is too long.

Seal fur is short and I have seen lots of it in secondhand stores, but my experience tells me not to use it anymore because it is difficult to sew: it lies so flat and the leather backing is quite heavy.

Also among my favorite furs for dolls is ermine, probably because I have rarely been able to buy it secondhand, and also because it is terribly expensive and usually shows up only on cuffs and collars, which must be pieced together to make anything substantial. Piecing fur is not difficult; you just have to make sure the fur on both pieces runs in the same direction before sewing them together.

The chinchilla coats you see herein all come from a piece of fur my old friend Kay Pace gave me when she saw one of the early rabbit fur coats. It was a strip perhaps six feet long and about fourteen inches wide, with a very fine thin leather backing and in excellent condition. She had paid seven dollars for it in a secondhand store; bought it maybe to use for a collar and cuffs on something. She had stashed it away for a long time and was reminded of it when I showed her a bunny coat. She was actually hesitant in offering it to me, thinking I wouldn't use it. Neither of us realized it was chinchilla at that time. My friend Edy identified it as such a couple of years later when she was looking through some doll clothes on my pegboard rack.

Our gorgeous Oriental Barbie® Doll model displays a rabbit fur coat worn casually over a pair of dark brown wool pants. She couldn't wear the hat that goes with this coat because of her elaborate hairdo.

The Beauty Secrets Christie® Doll models again her luxurious honey-colored mink coat. Her mauve lamé gown is trimmed with cotton braid, which has a tiny thread of mauve running through it.

133

The gorgeous Ballet Barbie® Doll models a luxurious mink coat worn over brown wool pants. This coat is a bit longer than the fur coat pattern calls for, because cutting it shorter would have been a waste of a lovely piece of fur. There was a little more than needed for one coat but not enough for two.

A close-up of the Hispanic Barbie® Doll in a short, blond mink coat. I just love this creamy color and have made several of these, since I was fortunate enough to be given some large scraps when a friend had her mink stole remodeled. The satin and velvet gown creates a lovely contrast for this particular coat.

Cutting and Sewing Fur

All my patterns for fur and leather are backed with cardboard so that I can draw around them directly on the leather. When cutting them out with my trusty X-Acto (#11 blade), I cut just inside the lines. I use a ball-point pen, and I certainly don't want those lines to transfer onto the lining later or to get gooped up in glue when I glue down the edges.

Have you looked at the fur coat pattern (Chapter Seven)? Both the coat and the sleeves for it may look like they have come from outer space if you've never seen a coat made this way before. But this pattern is the most economical in terms of the amount of fur used and in terms of seams. That's why the body of the coat is one piece; I have made fur coats with the standard coat pattern, but they are just too bulky and inflexible to look good on our tiny models.

Putting these pieces together is very simple. You just pin the sleeves in place, fur sides together, and stitch along the V-shaped line. I use a fairly small stitch, because long stitches tend to pull out when you turn your sleeve inside out, pulling it through with a crochet hook.

After you have attached both sleeves at the armhole, flip the coat over, and pin each sleeve (one at a time) together with the fur sides matching, and sew it up—not all the way, but just to the shoulder line. Pull the sleeve through with the crochet hook after checking your seam to make sure it's all right on both sides. You can either finish this seam by hand or on your sewing machine. If you do it by hand, my experience says use a whip-stitch to secure it. Then repeat the same operation on the opposite sleeve, and you have the makings of a real fur coat for your doll.

The last operation is to attach a collar all around, from one hem to the other, taking care that the fur on this long collar runs in the right direction both ways. You will want the fur to run downward, so that the bottom of the collar runs in neatly at the hemline, and if you cut this piece in half and turn one half around before stitching them together, your fur will run in both directions from the mid-seam. I hope that doesn't sound too complicated and that the explanation is clear.

Lining Fur Coats

You must cut your lining from the coat body pattern. I have given up lining sleeves, again because of unnecessary bulk. Cut your lining a tiny bit wider than the coat body so there will be an edge all around for turning under, and so that it is long enough for a hem. I don't cut out the V-shape for sleeves in the lining but just give it a straight cut from the top to the bottom edge of the sleeve inset. Then I pin this lining directly to the inside of the coat in a couple of places, at the top between the sleeves and again near the hem. You can fuse your hem before doing this after checking to make sure the lining is going to match up with about one-quarter-inch extra all around. I have fused all the edges occasionally if I'm in a hurry, but in general I don't because fused material is difficult to get a needle through, and you still have to attach the lining directly to the coat. This I do with a blanket stitch, so that all you see are tiny right-angle stitches if you look closely.

Be careful when you get to the armholes of the sleeves. You want to cover that inner seam entirely with your lining, so have a toothpick handy to push both the fur sleeve seam aside and also to form the lining edge. I whipstitch the lining fabric directly onto the leather seam. I am, of course, using a leather needle and a sturdy thimble at this point.

Are you more confused now than you were before you started?

One Step at a Time

Just take it one step at a time, and your confusion will evaporate as you move along from one step to the next. I didn't have a clue as to how my first fur coat would work out when I started, and only after I had finished did it occur to me that I could have made it first from fabric just to test out the fit. I really advise you very strongly to do that: try the pattern with any old fabric. Corduroy would be nice, because you could trim it later with leftover fur, but anything will do, if your purpose is just to assure yourself that it does come together in the end.

And let me emphasize the importance of having a toothpick or a wooden skewer right next to your sewing machine for pushing loose hairs on your fur out of the way as you are sewing. This is especially important when you sew the sleeves to the coat. Stray hairs need to be pushed back under the two layers of leather backing in order to make neat seams, and I haven't found anything more efficient than a toothpick.

Cellophane Tape

You can tape your pieces together with cellophane tape or even masking tape and sew right through it. The stitch line will probably cut your tape, which is fine, because you just pull it off after you're finished.

I would be delighted to hear from readers about any little tricks you may come up with in making wardrobes for your dolls. Necessity being the mother of invention, we all figure out ways to accomplish our ends, and I'm sure there are all kinds of wonderful, helpful hints lurking out there.

Fake Fur

Fake fur is treated like any other kind of napped fabric, because that is what it is. I use the fur coat pattern, rather than the standard coat pattern, for fake fur, but that is the only concession I make to its likeness to real fur.

Fake fur is a whole lot easier to find and much less expensive to buy than real fur. You must be careful about the backing on your fake fur, however. If it is too heavy or too stiff, the result won't be good. The two examples you see in the photographs, the fake leopard illustrated in Chapter Two and the fake seal seen here, are both very soft and pliable, and you can see how nicely they make up into doll clothes.

Sewing Leather

If you have never made clothes from leather, there is just one consideration for you to hang on to. And it's really nothing new to you if you have made any of the other doll clothes in this book, because I have emphasized this consideration repeatedly. Guess what? It is, of course, *weight* of the leather. If it's too heavy, it will drive you crazy; it won't drape well on the tiny models and will be too stiff even if you *can* get it on them.

Considering the number of glove-leather outfits on my models, you have probably picked up the impression that it's my absolutely favorite material to work with. That's true, and if you work with it, you will see why. Glove leather is very soft and very flexible, easy to cut and very easy to sew. You must use sharp leather needles both on the sewing machine and for sewing by hand, but they are the only special equipment you need. Ordinary thread works just fine and any old dull pair of scissors will cut it; not that I recommend using dull scissors for cutting anything, not even paper.

I have never used brand-new gloves for doll clothes, and I certainly don't recommend that you do. I just look in the glove drawer every time I am on one of my regular thrift shop runs, and I buy any pair of gloves (leather only) that costs less than five dollars, particularly if it is the long, over-the-elbow kind, and if there are more than one pair, I buy them all. I have a big surplus of gloves right now, because I get carried away on bargains, whether it's anything I need immediately or not. And who can resist a real bargain on a pair of fine kid or suede gloves for just a dollar or two? I have bought gloves for as little as fifty cents, and I just store them in Ziploc plastic bags until I get around to making something with them.

If you get used to handling glove leather, you will be able to tell a lot about other kinds of leather just by feel; by rubbing a piece of it between your thumb and forefinger. I have used lots of old suede that was in good condition and by good condition I don't mean only the surface but also the back. If the back looks dry and flaky, don't use it. That dryness

The Oriental Barbie ® Doll strolls out in a fake-fur leopard coat topped by a small brown wool hat. Her chocolate suede pants and smooth brown boots complete this outfit.

The Hispanic Barbie ® Doll steps out in a fake-fur coat worn over a red bouclé sweater and a plaid skirt. Her little fez hat picks up the color of her sweater. This fake fur is very soft and pliable, easy to cut and sew for the miniature fashion models.

will permeate and split suede wherever there is any pressure or pull.

The same thing is true of smooth leather. If the back side of it is cracked or flaky, don't use it. You'll be sorry if you do. And while we are on this subject, let me tell you where I have picked up some of the best smooth leather I've ever used. Better, even, than brand-new!

Used handbags are a terrific source for marvelous, soft, buttery leathers, absolutely perfect for doll clothes and accessories. The little shiny blue leather jacket in the centerfold is made from a small clutch purse I bought for less than a dollar in a Goodwill store. I didn't know exactly why I was buying it, or in fact, if it was even real leather, but I split all the seams when I got it home and it was (and is) terrific leather, in wonderful shape. I made two jackets and a vest from it. The brown suede pantsuit worn by the Black Barbie® Doll is made from purse leather, too.

Machine-Sewing Smooth Leather

You will find that sewing napped, or suede, leather is just like sewing fabric, but let me tell you about potential problems with sewing smooth leather on a machine. It won't always travel smoothly along on the feeder; it can get hung up *unless* you do one of two things. A leather foot will roll it smoothly along, but there is an easier solution than running out to buy a special foot for your machine. I discovered that using a piece of tissue paper on top of the leather will keep the action going. Then you just tear the paper loose from your stitches, after you have stitched right through it. The stitches perforate the paper so it tears easily. I have used facial tissue, but a smoother, harder-finish paper is better. Onionskin is perfect, and I always cut it into narrow strips just a little wider than my feeder foot. Once again necessity is the mother of invention.

I glue down both edges of a leather seam, not only because it makes a very nice and neat finish, but also because it helps shape the finished garment. I use leather glue or rubber cement for this delicate finishing work, spreading it carefully and then holding the

The Black Barbie® Doll shows off her soft, caramel-colored suede pantsuit worn over a ribbed T-shirt with a boat neck. Isn't she fetching?

The Ballet Barbie® Doll steps out in a red vinyl raincoat made from the standard coat pattern. There are a couple of small variations that you have probably noticed. The collar is not as long as the regular all-the-way-to-the-hem collar, and there are cuffs on the sleeves. The belt is finished off with a buckle from a watchband. Her white rain boots complete this charming rainy-day apparel.

Just a word about sewing vinyl. I peeled the stiff backing off the vinyl before cutting it out.

two edges together until they bond. It only takes a minute. Needless to say, this is how I finish hems and outer edges of all leather garments.

Leather Accessories

You have seen several leather accessories: purses, belts, and hats. They all have their own patterns (Chapter Eight), but let's talk for a moment about them.

The cowboy hat requires no sewing, and, in fact, I can't figure out a way to make it other than by gluing the parts together. I would welcome suggestions from any of my readers.

But the little leather hats made from glove fingers are another issue altogether. I must have a streak of incipient stinginess for that idea to have occurred to me. I just can't bear to waste good glove leather. First I tried to figure out how one split finger could be shaped into a hat, a sort of round hat with the seams going round and round. That didn't work, so I came up with the idea of using two split fingers and having the seams go up and down instead of around, leaving it open at the top and gathering it to form a little modified hourglass shape. Using pipe cleaners as a finishing touch was an idea left over from something I was working on a couple of years ago.

I guess one requirement of an aspiring designer of doll clothes is a willingness to try out things that just happen to be lying around. I use pipe cleaners to clean my typewriter and to stake up droopy plants, so it was just a natural extension of something I have been doing forever. Pipe cleaners are very useful for making hangers for doll clothes, too, in the absence of a store that stocks manufactured plastic hangers for Barbie® Doll clothes.

There isn't much to say about the little knit hats or the fur hats; I expect many of you have already figured out how to do them. They certainly don't need patterns.

We have already discussed the belts whenever they have been shown in Chapters Two, Three, and Four, but let me just caution you here not to get discouraged when you are making them of leather, because they are very tiny, narrow strips and sometimes (always!) they are difficult to thread through the buckle and to secure once they are through the tiny opening. You can't use a standard leather punch for the holes in the belt but must use something very sharp, like the point of embroidery scissors or a large needle. An awl is perfect, just as an ice pick is.

By the time this book goes to press, I expect to have found a better source for buying glove leather, such as buying seconds or irregulars directly from a glove manufacturer. If I have found such a source, my readers can write to me to find out where to get it directly, or else I will start buying and stockpiling this leather and I will sell it to you myself, for my cost plus mailing and handling.

These models are posed to show the different effects of fur on the same basic long brown brocade coat. These coats are shown to best advantage when the models' hair is up, rather than hanging down over the fur collar.

Chapter Seven

Coats, Jackets, Capes, Stoles, and Shawls

COATS ARE, OF COURSE, central to any complete wardrobe. When I designed the very first coat in this collection, it was not from divine inspiration or even from a consuming passion for coats and other outerwear. I designed the coat because I couldn't find a ready-made Barbie® Doll coat in any of the toy stores of San Francisco, which is not to say that Mattel was not producing coats. I *have* seen coats on the racks of doll clothes since that time.

If I had been able to find one then, I probably would have taken it apart, or at least figured out how it was made, and copied it in a better fabric, but since I couldn't find one, I started looking at pattern books. I looked at commercial doll clothes patterns first, of course, but found nothing I liked. Worse, I thought, than not being able to find a coat pattern was not finding one for a jacket, which could have been modified and extended into a coat.

So I designed my own pattern, made some coats and jackets, worked out the bugs in the pattern, and finally arrived at one standard pattern that can be used for a long evening coat, a short daytime coat, or a jacket.

The Formal Evening Coat

Let's talk about the long coats first, since they are the most difficult to make. As you can see from the pictures, I used very elegant materials, mostly brocades, which bring special problems to the seamstress just by the nature of their loose weave. They all ravel easily; they are slippery and fragile fabrics. I have ripped out sleeve stitching more than once as I pulled the sleeve through with a crochet hook.

Therefore I caution you to do this very carefully when you are working with delicate or fragile material. Never try to yank the sleeve through. I have found that a sort of push-pull action gets the best result; pushing with the eraser end of a pencil as you pull gently with the crochet hook.

By the same token, once your coat is made, you must be very careful when you put it on your doll. Straight-arm dolls are easier to deal with than the other, bent-arm ones, of course, because it is possible to push the arms straight back and slip the arms into the sleeves easily. You can see that I have mastered the art of slipping long-sleeved coats over bent arms, but I can tell you it is difficult and requires very careful easing on of the coat.

Also, whether you have a straight- or bent-armed doll, her thumb is likely to get hung up in anything it goes through. The answer to that is to wrap a small scrap of fabric around the whole hand before inserting it into anything it can catch on. I've used cellophane tape to cover hands, but that's more trouble than it's worth. Tissues also work if they don't tear going through.

One of the Black Barbie ® Dolls has flexible arms—I forget which one—but she is absolutely ideal, and I don't understand why Mattel doesn't make all their dolls with this kind of arm. I would *never* buy a bent-arm doll for a child under ten years of age, unless I was prepared to spend a whole lot of time teaching the kid how to manipulate those arms into and out of clothes. Since they are difficult for me to manipulate, I figure any child who hasn't developed very fine manual dexterity would be frustrated by the effort to get sleeves on and off without ruining clothes. The Catch-22 of this is that all the beautiful ethnic Barbie ® Dolls have bent arms; Parisian, Scottish, Hispanic, Italian, and Oriental. Some of the Black Barbie ® Dolls do, too.

My choice would be for flexible arms that bend like most of the legs do, not for stiffly straight arms like the Malibu Barbie ® and Malibu Christie ® Dolls, and certainly not for those permanently bent arms on most of the dolls. The Ballet Barbie ® Doll has the same stiffly straight arms as the Malibu Dolls, but her arms and hands are prettier for some reason. Look at the picture of the Ballet Barbie ® Doll modeling the black sequined-bodice evening dress. Doesn't she have pretty arms and hands? Is that a function of being a ballerina? Maybe the Barbie ® Doll lovers of America should petition Mattel to make our favorite dolls with the kind of arm *we* prefer.

But let's get back to our discussion of making long, fancy, opulent, sumptuous, elegant, gorgeous coats for our dolls. First off, I'm going to suggest you make your first one of a fabric somewhat less troublesome than brocade, something like velveteen or corduroy, just to get the feel of making this garment and to assure yourself that it will work out perfectly.

I hope I never sound as if I am talking down to you, but my memories of failures are still very close, and I'd like to spare you that, if possible. On the other hand, if you are an experienced seamstress, I shouldn't presume to give you advice of any sort. You can probably give me some!

THE SINGLE-PIECE COAT

You surely don't need to be told again that you can eliminate the seam down the outside of the sleeve by cutting out the coat on a fold corresponding to the shoulder-sleeve line of the pattern, and then cutting the front of the coat open, or not cutting it open until after the side and underarm seams are sewn. You can see coats made by both methods on the models, but in general, I try to keep seams to a minimum whenever I am using a loose-weave material. It is a good idea to secure the edges of all seams with a medium-tight zigzag stitch as well, for added stability.

The single-piece coat pattern is only one-quarter of a complete coat, with instructions to cut the back on a fold and to cut two fronts. In order to have a full pattern to place on the fold for no top seam on sleeves, you will have to cut out that half pattern on a folded piece of paper. You can do that easily by tracing the pattern on a big enough piece of paper to fold before you cut the traced pattern out, and, of course, do the same with the jacket pattern.

To Line or Not to Line

I don't line every single long formal coat but only do so when my fabric is very sheer or very fragile, if I want to add some body to the material. Since I never line sleeves, my pattern for a lining looks different from the coat it is used for. I have not supplied a pattern for a lining, because it would be an insult to the reader's intelligence.

The sleeveless sequined evening coat you see on the Italian Barbie ® Doll is sleeveless for

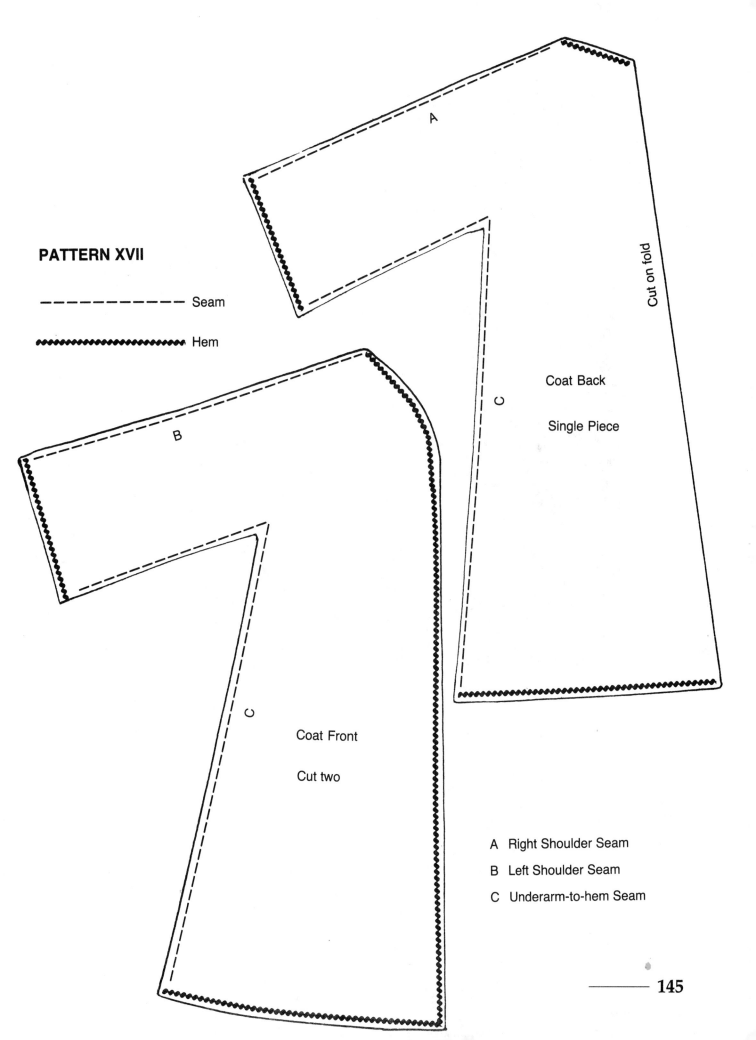

PATTERN XVII

– – – – – – – – Seam

✦✦✦✦✦✦✦✦✦✦✦✦ Hem

A

Cut on fold

Coat Back

Single Piece

C

B

C

Coat Front

Cut two

A Right Shoulder Seam

B Left Shoulder Seam

C Underarm-to-hem Seam

145

The Oriental Barbie® Doll models a silver brocade evening coat here. This is very stiff, unyielding fabric, which had to be pinned together along the front edge to get a good frontal shot that shows the lamé edge. She was wearing a dress under this coat when we first posed her, which we removed in order to make the coat hang straight.

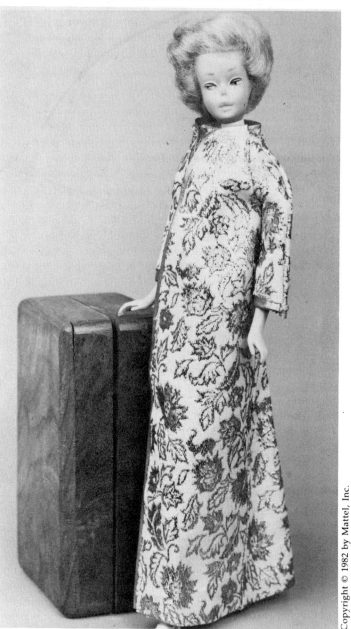

This model is a Barbie® Doll almost, if not actually, twenty years old. Her rather brassy-looking bubble hairdo betrays her age. The coat she is wearing is not made from our pattern, but very well could be. I don't like the set-in sleeves because they are much harder to make and, in fact, are downright dangerous to make with this sort of fabric, which ravels terribly. The minimum number of seams should have been used. This is a very beautiful brocade, don't you agree?

The Hispanic Barbie® and the Italian Barbie® Dolls make an attractive pair, don't they? Dressed for an evening out, the sitting model wears a black fake-fur coat trimmed with white rabbit fur. The standing model shows off a sequined, fuchsia-colored sleeveless brocade evening coat trimmed with wide bands of black velvet. Her silver lamé dress and stretchy Lurex bodice make this a stunning combination.

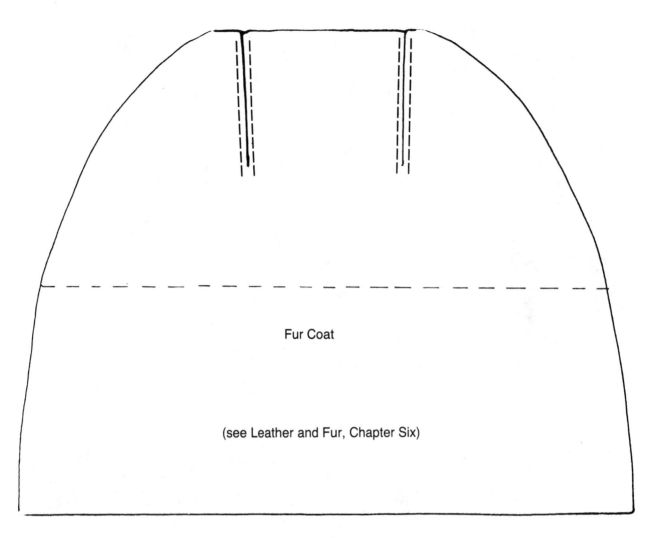

Fur Coat

(see Leather and Fur, Chapter Six)

PATTERN XVIII

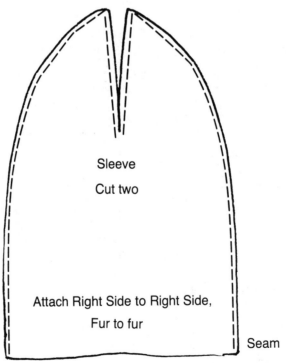

Sleeve

Cut two

Attach Right Side to Right Side,
Fur to fur

Seam

one reason only: I ran out of fabric. There was only a small piece left over, and I was darned if I'd waste it, so I made a sleeveless coat and made wide bands of black velvet to jazz it up a bit.

USING THE FUR-COAT PATTERN FOR LONG COATS

There are no side seams to be seen on some of the long brocade coats that are posed on dolls in profile. When I know in advance that I'm going to use a broad band of fur to trim a long formal coat, I prefer to use the fur-coat pattern as one way of minimizing seams. Of course, that means there will be an outside seam on the top of the sleeve, so you are exchanging one problem for another, and if you do it this way, you must remember to be careful in pulling the sleeves through.

Lining a coat made this way is very easy. You just cut both the coat and the lining out at the same time, using the coat pattern. Then place the right sides of the material together, stitch all around the side and bottom edges, turn it rightside out, and attach your sleeves. What could be easier?

Finishing Edges with Lamé Strips

You have doubtless taken note of the many edges of long, formal coats finished with lamé or satin ribbon strips. This is a very simple operation. You will need a one-half inch strip of ribbon, about twenty-two inches to two feet in length to be absolutely safe. Pin right sides together directly on the coat, along the edge all the way around, and then stitch it together, leaving about one-quarter inch at each end to be turned under. I don't actually pin this strip any longer because I have done so many of them. And I try not to use pins in any case with lamé because of the little pin-holes left in the fabric. I prefer alligator clamps.

Finishing this edge on the inside of the coat is just a little more complicated. I use fusion tape, which I press carefully into place, and then if I want a really pretty finish, I will fuse narrow lace over that exposed edge. I

The Parisian Barbie® Doll takes a turn in the same long luxurious mink coat you have seen on a couple of other models. I like to show the different contrasts with different colors of hair—blond, black, and in this instance, reddish-gold. The Parisian Barbie® Doll is a strawberry blond, I believe.

149

also fuse wider lace over the inside seams to add an elegant finishing touch. This final fusion adds body to any garment, so it's a very good thing to keep in mind. Fusing lace over hems is a wonderful way to make a wide skirt stand out as if there were an invisible hoop underneath.

Attaching Fur to Brocade

When you opt for a fur trim on a long formal coat there are several decisions to make before you even begin to cut out your pattern. Which coat pattern will you use? I almost always go for the fur-coat pattern for all the reasons already stated and for one yet unstated. The front and neck edges where you attach the fur directly to the material are rounded, and the overlap from right side to left side is less. When I have used the regular coat pattern and later decided to add fur, I have always had to trim the edge by about one-half inch, because the garment is simply too bulky to add fur.

To Glue or Not to Glue

We have discussed the virtues of gluing fur to leather. It is also possible to glue fur directly to fabric. It will look terrific at first, but the bond won't be as good as it is with leather, and you will probably end up having to glue it back together when it separates. If you don't mind such little repair jobs, go ahead and glue it.

I prefer to sew the fur strip directly to the fabric. I use either a plain old whipstitch or a blanket stitch, and of course, a leather needle.

I match my thread to the color of the fur rather than the color of the fabric, because I know that if it doesn't look absolutely terrific on the inside edge of the fabric, I can always sew a strip of lace along that edge to cover it. Of course, you can't fuse anything after the fur is attached, because the amount of heat required to fuse fabrics together would damage the fur.

It Ain't Easy!

If all these instructions and counterinstructions strike terror in your heart, let me reassure you that most mistakes and disasters can be salvaged. I have blown more than one sleeve, but that's really a tiny disaster as long as you have more fabric. It is a simple matter to replace the sleeve; it takes a little time, but who's running a marathon?

Everyone I have met who makes doll clothes does it for fun and for the satisfaction of creating something beautiful. And if you are reading this, I will guarantee you are a creative person, because if you weren't, you'd only be looking at the pretty pictures.

At the same time, I can't tell you that making coats is a lead-pipe cinch. Coats are probably the most difficult garment in this book, but patience and care pay off in the end when you have created a beautiful and functional garment. Just working with these tiny pattern pieces requires a special skill not possessed by everyone. I think anyone who wants to develop such a skill can, however. Practice and patience are the answers. I didn't consider myself an expert when I started all this, and I still don't think I am really a hotshot seamstress. It's for fun and for playing out our fantasies!

One last admonition before we go on to the street coats and jackets. Don't limit yourself to the kinds of fabrics you see in this book. Use your imagination, indulge your own taste, and try everything!

EVERYDAY COATS

You have seen two fake-fur street coats, a black Persian lamb coat trimmed with mink, a suede coat trimmed with rabbit fur, a gray flannel coat, and a red vinyl raincoat. They are all made from the same basic coat patterns, but they look very different from one another, don't they? A little variation here and there can really change the look of a basic pattern, even something as simple as a change in fabric, a tie belt versus a buckled one, a long

The Parisian Barbie® and Malibu Christie® Dolls compare their long, brocade evening coats trimmed with two very different furs. The chocolate-brown coat, worn by the beautiful blond model, is trimmed with almost-black rabbit fur, the strips perhaps a tiny bit too wide. The white coat, which dips slightly at the mid-back point, is trimmed with a very lush, brownish-gray mink.

I include this shot of Your First Barbie ® Doll in a Persian lamb coat trimmed with mink only because the coat looks terrific even in such a silly pose. Since the doll's legs don't bend at the knee, she should have been standing.

collar versus a short one. Accessories in different colors and materials will take you another step further.

These everyday coats are made exactly the same way the long formal coats are; they are just shorter. I am sorry there are no fur-trimmed basic wool coats in this collection; I have made many of them, and they're darling. I use narrower strips of fur for daytime coats than for the luxurious evening wear, as you can see for yourself on the suede sporty coat with fur collar and cuffs and on the black Persian lamb daytime coat, which is trimmed with mink.

Because of their bulk, the daytime coats can only be worn over a sleeveless blouse or dickie. They look terrific over a narrow skirt or any kind of pants, but especially the straight narrow ones.

THE JACKETS

You have seen a great variety of jackets in the pictures of this book. I had hoped to increase that variety by designing a double-breasted reefer or pea jacket as well as doing a very traditional type of blazer, but press time comes very quickly when you are writing a book against a deadline, and I just didn't get around to them. Perhaps next time. The variety that does exist is mostly demonstrated by the use of different fabric combinations and colors.

If you will keep in mind the thought that a jacket is just a very small coat, especially if you have already made a coat before attempting a jacket, then I think you will have no problems.

But perhaps it would make better sense at this point to tell you the problems I have encountered, so you can avoid them. Fitting these tiny garments to the body of the model is the main problem I have had, but the way to beat that one is to use very soft, very flexible material that drapes easily on the doll's figure. When a jacket is too loose or too bulky, I have split the back right up the middle, removed some fabric, and made a seam there. When shaping the two front edges of any jacket, or preparing those edges for whatever trim I

This Barbie® Doll models a suede coat with fur collar and cuffs. The fur used to trim this coat is clearly too long. A very simple coat for an amateur to make; the basic coat of suede is made first, then strips of fur are simply glued directly to the leather.

PATTERN XIX

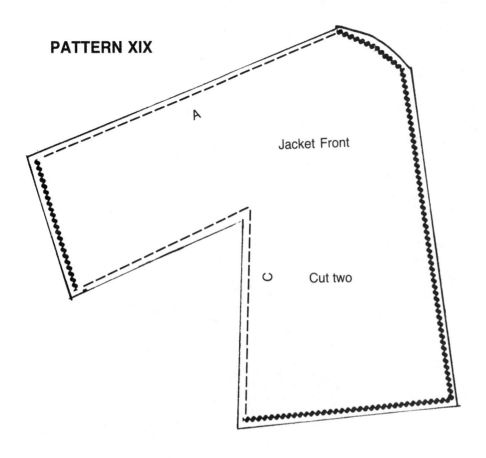

A Right Shoulder Seam

B Left Shoulder Seam

C Underarm-to-hem Seam

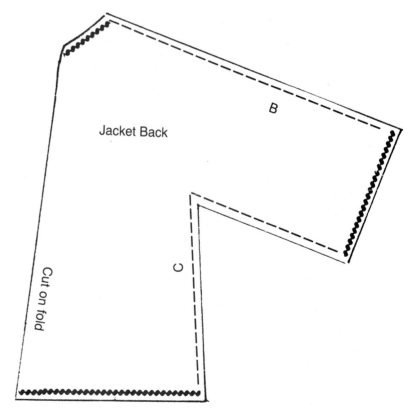

154 ——————

plan to use, I don't hesitate to cut off excess material.

You can see from a very quick glance through the pictures that the jackets fit well, and in many cases even seem to hug the body of the model. A couple of the wool ones are a little bulky, but that is due more to the nature of the fabric than to a faulty pattern. There are no darts in any of my jackets, which would make for a better fit but would complicate a very simple pattern.

I don't believe we need to go into the mechanics of cutting out and putting together a jacket here, since it is just a simplified version of all the coats and robes (Chapter Four). After you have made any one of these garments, you can make them all, and you won't need instructions each time on how to achieve your own finished product.

Materials and Color Combinations

Shall we briefly consider the variety of materials shown on the models, and secondarily the color combinations we have used?

You have seen many wool jackets. They are all made of the lightest-weight wool I could find, and they are trimmed with suede cloth or with a solid-color wool to complement the weave.

You have seen linen, velvet, and Lurex jackets, and of course, several glove-leather jackets, both in pantsuits and in regular business suits for the executive woman.

Technically speaking, we should count the bed jackets and pajama jackets, too. Made from nylon tricot and from quilted cotton, as well as from quilted synthetic fabric, they all demonstrate the versatility of our basic jacket pattern.

Now how much can we really say about color choices? I think not very much, because it is always a case of personal taste or of what is available. It should be pretty clear to the reader what my choices are and how my taste runs. I like primary colors very much, but I can't resist delicate pastels either. My taste is eclectic, and I indulge every little facet.

I hope you will do the same. Indulge all your favorite fantasies, and have fun!

The Pretty Secrets Christie® Doll displays a little lace stole backed by deep maroon velvet, which blends nicely with her mauve lamé dress. This particular dress might be improved by the removal of the braid trim around the hem.

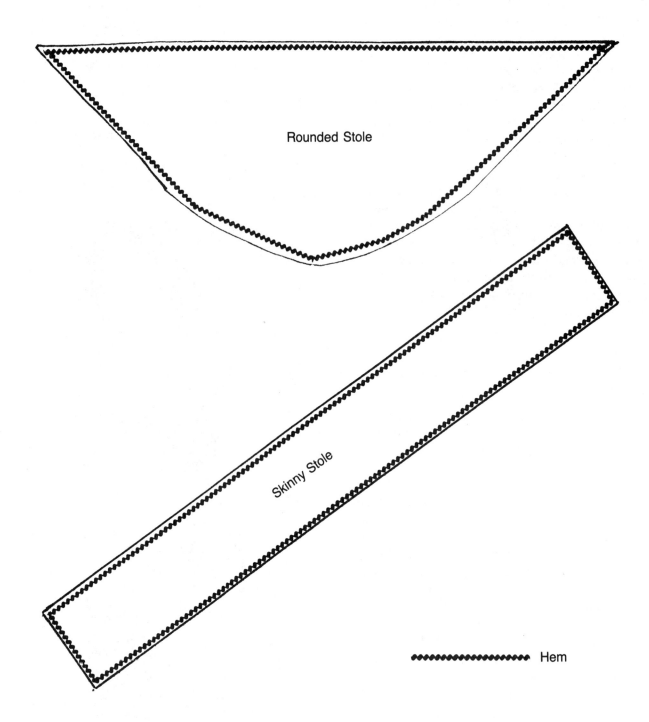

Rounded Stole

Skinny Stole

●●●●●●●●●●●●●●●● Hem

PATTERN XX

PATTERN XXI

------- Seam

∿∿∿∿ Hem

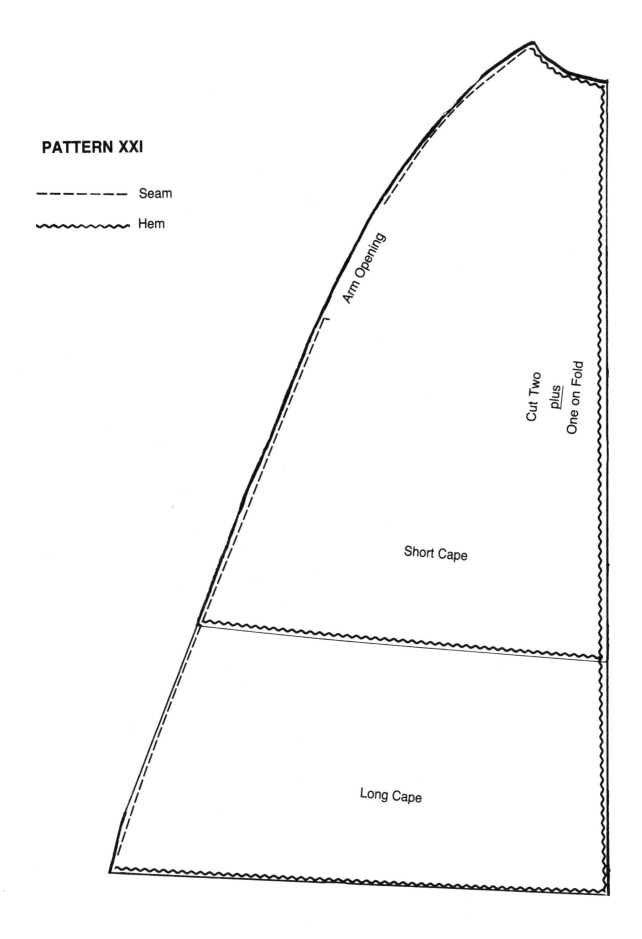

Arm Opening

Cut Two
plus
One on Fold

Short Cape

Long Cape

CAPES, STOLES, AND SHAWLS

These elegant evening wraps are very simple to make, but if you choose opulent materials as I have, then you must be very careful, even though the patterns look as though they are so simple they couldn't possibly be ruined.

And I admit it would be difficult to ruin a cape. I have, however, ruined one, a beautiful red velvet one. The way I spoiled it was just a little short of total idiocy, since I had plenty of the fabric and could have tested my plan of gluing fur directly to the velvet. I didn't test it; I ruined it. So much for that; don't ever try to glue anything to the napped surface of velvet.

Shawls and stoles can be spoiled only by cutting them too small. Or at least that's the only way I've ruined them. I'm sure I haven't exhausted all the possibilities.

If you cut a shawl too small, you can always add a lacy flounce or even make a self-ruffle of the same fabric if you have enough. As you can see from the pattern, shawls are just triangular pieces of fabric, edged with lace or a ruffle. If you use fur for the edge, be sure the material is strong enough to support the weight of the fur. A chiffon shawl will not support that much weight, but velvet or heavy satin will. Practical considerations.

I have made capes, long and short, of satin, brocade, fake fur, and velvet. I am only showing velvet in this collection because I have long since given up making capes of any other material. Take a look for yourself; could this blue velvet cape possibly be improved on?

The Parisian Barbie ® Doll models a long blue velvet evening cape trimmed with white rabbit fur. This fur is not glued on but whipstitched to the edge of the cape. Isn't she regal? A shorter version can be seen in the opening of Chapter Seven.

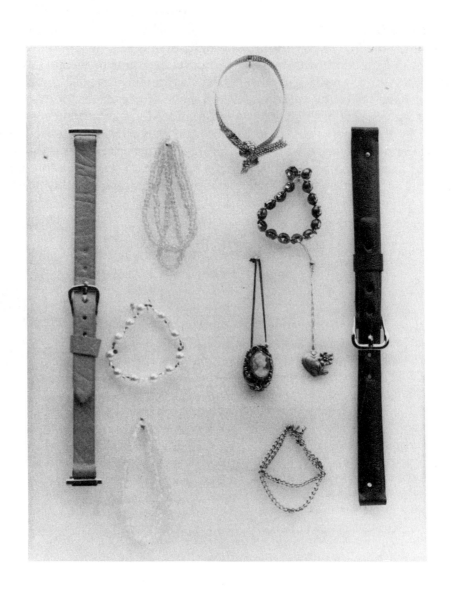

Chapter Eight

The Accessories

AN ACCESSORY IS, by definition, something extra, useful, or decorative, but not essential, according to my *Oxford American Dictionary*. I think that covers everything we have included in this chapter; belts, hats, scarves, dickies, and, of course, the jewelry. They are all used to accent particular garments and to change a basic look into a more finished look.

SCARVES AND DICKIES

Let's start with the scarves and the dickies, since they have all been used to fill in necklines that looked a little bare. The scarves can be either squares of fabric, or a triangular-shaped piece, or even a long, skinny piece. You can figure out your own dimensions; a pattern would insult your intelligence!

The dickie is just a very short blouse, always totally without sleeves, and is marked off on the basic blouse pattern (Chapter Three). You must make your own decisions about what sort of neckline you want; scoop, cowl, turtleneck, or whatever. Personally I believe it is so little trouble to make a complete blouse and takes such a little bit more material that it's hardly worth making dickies. I did only a couple of them for this book to show some variety.

BELTS AND JEWELRY

The belts are all made the same way: use a narrow piece of leather, ultrasuede, or fabric, fold it down the middle, and stitch the edges together. If it is a tie belt rather than a buckled belt, it must be a bit longer, but I don't need to tell you that, do I?

Running it through the tiny buckle can be a real drag, as you will soon find out for yourself, but once you get it through, you can take a couple of stitches to secure it, or glue it if you're very careful or don't mind replacing the glue when it pulls loose. I make the holes for the buckle with an awl, but if you don't have an awl (or an ice pick), a pair of pointed embroidery scissors will do the trick.

The jewelry is very simple stuff: tiny necklaces of seed pearls or little chains, a lavaliere with a cameo (pierced earring) pendant, and a seed pearl bracelet. There are also a couple of bangle bracelets made from wicker loops that look a bit like a bamboo bracelet.

If you secure the necklaces, you are going to wonder how to get them off and on the doll, right? I haven't been able to come up with anything, except to take your doll's head off. Sounds yukky, doesn't it? All Barbie® Doll heads come off easily unless there is a panel in the doll's back to make her wink (the Western Barbie® Doll) or wave her arms.

A collection of purses and handbags: Left to right, on top, a tiny bag made of some medallion braid. The next bag is of the paisley velvet also used for a dickie on the model wearing the green glove-leather pantsuit. The shoulder bag on the right is made from a piece of already topstitched vinyl that I thought would be perfect, and so it is. The fourth one, bottom row, is of the same topstitched vinyl, with a shorter strap. And I don't know where the little corduroy clutch bag came from!

Three scarves made from leftover fabric used in
the suits worn by the models.

You've seen this outfit before, but here it is modeled again with a tam made from a matching burgundy suede cloth. The soft and flexible skirt is now complemented by the soft and flexible look of the tam.

Look at the benefits this jacket sweater made from baby-mitten fabric has gained from a belt made from a watchband. The leather Stetson hat certainly makes this model ready for a casual day of fun.

THE HATS

We have shown several kinds of hats; the cowboy Stetson, the knit stocking cap, the little gored hat, the beret or tam o'shanter. We also include instructions for the chef's top hat. I should mention the fur hat, too, which is actually nothing more than a narrow band of fur fitted to the doll's head. This should be no wider than one-half inch, lest it overpower your doll's face.

The pattern for the Stetson is the most difficult of these. There are four pieces to this pattern: the brim, the rounded part of the crown, the top of the crown, and the hatband. The entire hat is glued. First you glue the ends of the rounded crown together, overlapping them. Then push it into the brim and glue the under-edge to the brim, pinching them together until they bond. The top of the crown is inserted into the crown round, and if you have a plastic cap the right size, place your hat on it for the next stage. Or do as I did and make a little hat form from a piece of styrofoam or cork to hold your Stetson. Then make a thin line of glue around the inside top edge of your crown and pinch it down onto the crown top.

Voilà! A cowboy Stetson of leather—I use *only* leather for these hats. Your last step is to glue the hatband on, covering the line of insertion where the crown meets the brim. I cross the ends of the hatband in back to make a little X.

The stocking cap is made from a piece of knit fabric, zigzag-stitched all around to stop (or at least impede) raveling, then sewn up the side and across the top. I roll a little brim and secure it with a couple of hand stitches, then make the pompon from the same fabric. This is easy; you just cut out a circle of about one-inch circumference, gather it and attach it to your cap.

The gored hat is made from either two or four gores—your choice. The smaller one on the pattern is for the four-gored one and the large one is for a two-gored hat. You have seen examples of both in the pictures; I prefer the four-gored one, as it looks more like a professional job. Last you attach your brim, stitching it directly to the edge of the hat, right sides together, and then tucking it inside, where you can either secure it with a few stitches, or if you are using leather, as I have for most of my hats, glue it.

The beret and tam are made from exactly the same pattern, the only difference being that the tam has a pompon. A very simple pattern, it is just two cut-out circles sewn right sides together after cutting a round hole in one of the circles to fit the doll's head. Turn it right side out, and you have a beret. I use mostly leather or a nonraveling fabric like suede cloth for these hats, so it isn't necessary to finish the cut edge that pulls down on the doll's head. If you have to finish that edge, you have several options. I just use a zigzag stitch for it because it won't show when it's on the doll.

Now for the chef's hat—and that's an awful name for such a smart hat, but it's at least descriptive. This hat pattern has three pieces; the brim, the rounded crown, which looks very large for such a small hat, but which has a line of stitching in front to shape it, and the actual top of the crown. The brim is longer than the crown piece, because this hat ties in back after all the pieces are together. I am sorry I didn't make several examples of this little hat for you to see, but by the time I realized I needed more of them, it was too late.

I urge you to experiment with hats. They are a lot of fun and they certainly lend a finished look to any outfit.

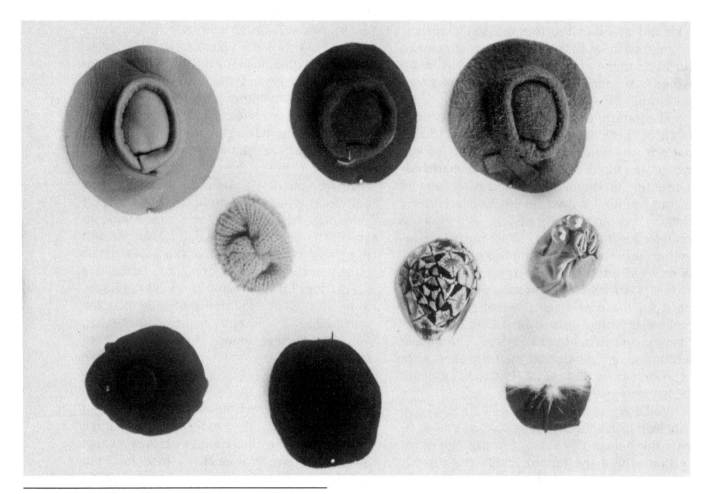

This is a collection of hats you have seen on various models. In the top row are cowboy Stetsons, made of leather. Just below them is a knit stocking cap with a pompon on top. In that same row, but slightly off center, is the little matching medallion braid hat (it goes with the bag of the same fabric). This hat is edged with a narrow strip of lamé all around the brim. Then you see the little teal-blue, stretchy nylon hat that is part of a suit of the same fabric. In the bottom row, from left to right, is a scarlet beret with a same-fabric covered button. It looks more like a tam o'shanter than a beret. Then there is a dark brown beret that looks like a beret, and finally a little leather skullcap with a puff of rabbit fur on the side.

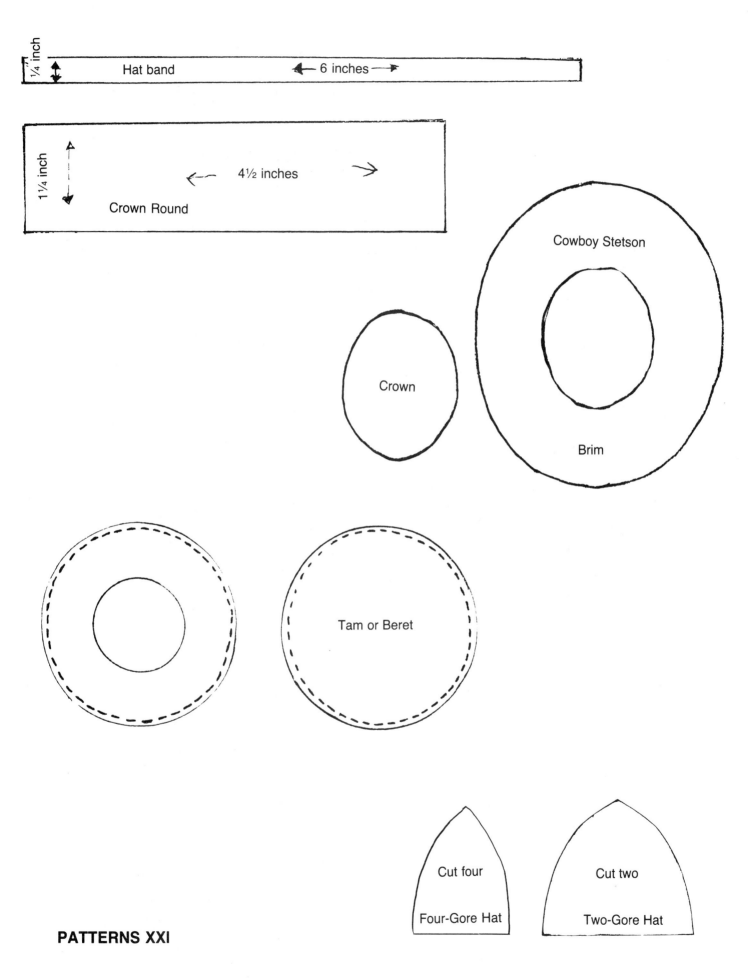

¼ inch

Hat band ◄─ 6 inches ─►

1¼ inch

◄─ 4½ inches ─►

Crown Round

Cowboy Stetson

Crown

Brim

Tam or Beret

Cut four

Four-Gore Hat

Cut two

Two-Gore Hat

PATTERNS XXI

Chapter Nine

The Wedding Dresses

Y OU DON'T NEED TO be told how much fun I had making these wedding dresses, do you? The results speak for themselves.

Actually I could go on forever making wedding dresses; they are the ultimate expression of fantasy ideals.

Three of the five wedding dresses are made from the basic gown pattern—they are variations of the same dress, which is my copy of Princess Diana's dress. You can see from these variations on a theme that there are almost infinite possibilities for improvising on a basic pattern. I have used the same white lining satin for two of them, but the necklines are quite different, and so are the skirt treatments.

The other one is made from heavy satin in a creamy ecru shade and is still different from the two white ones. The skirt is as wide as I could make it of this heavy satin—I would have liked to make it even fuller, but the tiny waist of the model doll puts a definite limitation on how wide any skirt can be, as you well know if you have made clothes for this doll.

The other two dresses are entirely figments of my imagination, and I could not give you a pattern for either of them for that reason. Let's talk about the one with lace flounces first.

If you will take a close look you can see that those lace flounces are doubled. I bought this lace at a flea market for a couple of dollars, which I thought was extravagant! There were about 1½ yards of it, already gathered, just waiting for my imagination to start working. I put it away for a few months, out of sight, but then I came across it one day and decided such beautiful lace just cried out to be used in something absolutely gorgeous.

So I made a long skirt, quite full, from some shiny white satin, pinned two rows of the lace to the skirt, and tried it on a doll to see what the effect was. Stunning, of course!

Well, I sat there racking my brain for an idea of a top for this dress, thinking how awful it would be to cut into the lace for a traditional dress with just a little trim on the bodice, fooling around with the lace the whole while, draping it this way and that. It suddenly occurred to me to cut armholes in the underlayer and see how that would drape. Again the result speaks for itself, doesn't it? The only thing left was to see if this rather heavy lace could be draped into a veil. It's not as pretty as the other veil, but not bad for a couple of hours of just fooling around.

And speaking of the other veil, it was also made after the gown it is worn with, to complement the gown.

Two imitations of the Lady Di wedding dress, where I took some artistic license. The skirts are too narrow to be good imitations, and the skirt trims are very different from the cream-colored imitation (see page 166). These are made of lining satin, which doesn't have enough body to support a very full skirt. The bodices are adapted from the same blouse pattern that was used for all the street dresses, with a V-neck on the right and a modest scoop on the left. The sleeves are as faithful to the original as I could make them.

Sorry I can't offer you a pattern for this fancy beaded wedding gown, because it was put together in bits and pieces in order to get the maximum mileage out of the beading on the fabric. The veil is very easy to copy, of course; a simple, round, open crown to which the veil is gathered.

This very ornate dress, embroidered with seed pearls, is made from a scrap left over from an actual wedding gown, and it certainly didn't work out as quickly as the other one. I had to cut the skirt very carefully in order to get the whole embroidered pattern on the front of the skirt, and as if that wasn't enough painstaking work for one dress, I also had to come up with a way to incorporate the pattern into the sleeves. I settled on less than the whole embroidery, which worked out all right.

The bodice is made from another piece of fabric, plain white silk crepe, substantial enough to hang the embroidery on and to attach the sleeves to. The skirt is fully lined with the same white silk crepe, so it won't be a see-through wedding gown. Not that I object to see-through clothes; it just seems incongruous in a wedding gown! The skirt is quite narrow, because the fabric is very stiff.

In lieu of providing patterns for these two fancy wedding gowns, let me just say one thing. You can do it, too, if you let your imagination go, and try everything once.

This dress, modeled by the Parisian Barbie ® Doll would be very simple to copy, since it is just a white satin skirt with two double flounces of gathered lace. The top, which can scarcely be called a bodice, is another length of double lace, with sleeves cut into the underlayer and the top layer draped around the bride's neck and over her shoulders. The veil is a third piece of the double lace, pinned to the doll's hair. Improvisation from start to finish!

Here you see Barbie® modeling my Lady Diana look-alike dress made from creamy ecru satin, rather stiff, but still manageable for this tiny model.

A close-up of the imitation Lady Di gowns, worn by Italian Barbie® Dolls, one with an upswept hairdo and one with her hair down. I am very fond of the rosettes on the skirt of the V-neck dress—pride of creation, undoubtedly. I didn't know whether they would work well or not. I'll try one with smaller rosettes next time. Don't you just love the lacy flounces around the collars? And the big sleeves?

Isn't this a terrific shot of all five wedding gowns together? From the top model, clockwise: The Hispanic Barbie® Doll models my Lady Diana look-alike dress. On her left is the Golden Dreams Barbie® Doll, posing in a completely different style of wedding gown. This dress has a narrow skirt, long puffed sleeves, and a very full veil.

Next are the two Italian Barbie® Dolls modeling two more variations of the Lady Diana dress. You can see the small differences if you look closely, and you can also see that their hairstyles are different.

The Parisian Barbie® Doll, on the left, models my own creation, conceived out of a need for a pretty use for the beautiful double rows of lace.

All these dresses, ornate as they seem, are easy to make. Any competent seamstress could have designed all of them.

Chapter Ten

Styling Your Doll's Hair

*I*TRUST YOU HAVE noticed the models are shown with a variety of different hair styles. Here is a detail of one of the pictures from the chapter on wedding dresses with two Italian Barbies®, one of whom has an upswept hairdo, while the other one wears her hair long and flowing, just the way she arrived from the store.

Obviously, different kinds and styles of apparel call for different, more or less formal hairstyles. Pigtails hanging down their backs would not be appropriate for models dressed in lamé evening gowns and mink coats, right? Nor would an elaborately curled and coiffed

model look proper in a jogging suit. That is, unless the gates of a well-known mental institution were the backdrop for such a picture.

I used to have a lot of trouble with the hair of these little models. Then I rediscovered the efficacy of good old American hairspray, that staple cosmetic device of every proper American lady of the sixties and early seventies who wore the regulation bubble hairdo. Mine would collapse into limp ringlets unless I sprayed it stiff as a board. God help anyone who dared to pat me on the head. He'd recoil as if his hand had gone into a nest of vipers!

Out of the Mouths of Babes

Jenny was spending the weekend with me a few years back when she was still capable of frittering away an entire afternoon playing with Barbie ® dolls. I forget how it came up, but she asked me to help her make a fancy hairdo, so I sat on the floor with her, brushing, combing, and pinning doll hair into fancy ringlets, chignons, and French twists. The problem was that the hair would fall right down when we took out the pins (we were securing the ringlets with straight pins stuck right into the dolls' skulls).

Then Jenny asked how come I didn't have any hairspray around. Ah, inspiration! We went to the store and loaded up with spray and the tiniest hair clips we could find. Bobby pins and hairpins are just a total waste of time: too big and too hard to manipulate. But let me tell you, those little clippies really get the job done!

We learned that with the aid of hairspray and a tiny hair clip, we could turn any straight-haired doll into a ringleted Scarlett O'Hara. Long ringlets are harder than anything else, but we found that if we made ponytails on each side of a doll's head, just above her ears, then wrapped a strand of her own hair around and over the rubber band holding the ponytail, and gave it a little spritz from the spray can, we were on our way.

Ringlets for a Southern Belle

The hair in each ponytail must be divided into equal portions for the number of ringlets you want on each side. That can be anything from three to five, and you should slip a hair clip on each section to keep them out of the way. I use a fat straw or a pencil or pen for brushing the hair around, then snap a clip on the curl at the top and at the bottom. You can spray them individually as you make them, but I prefer to spray all of them at once when I'm finished. And I spray the inside of the curl as well as the outside—almost saturate it.

Let it dry. You can help it along with a blow dryer, but be careful not to blow the hair loose from the clip. When it is thoroughly dry, remove the clip and give it one more quick overall spritzing.

Voilà! A southern belle.

The French Twist

This coiffure couldn't be easier, though you may have to trim a little of your doll's hair, because too much hair makes for a bulky twist.

Brush the hair smoothly back over your doll's ears, give it one good tight twist to secure it, clip into place, and spritz. It looks ghastly at this point, but that can't be helped. Let it dry, then remove the clips and roll it into place, securing again with a clip. I give it a good healthy blast and leave it alone until it is thoroughly dry.

The side twists you see on a couple of the models are made roughly the same way and look terrific no matter how bulky they turn out to be.

A couple of cautionary notes here. Don't cut your doll's hair unless you absolutely have to. Once that hair is cut, it's irrevocably gone; it won't grow back. I try to shield the models' faces when I'm giving their hair the old blast, because that stuff looks nasty on faces! It will wipe off with a damp cloth, so we're not talking about a potential disaster, but an ounce of prevention, etc.

So You Prefer a Fancy Upsweep?

The upswept coiffures are the easiest of all. Really! Depending on where you place your ponytail, you can end up with a tousled look or a very sleek and sophisticated look. You can have lots of little curls or a few nice fat ones. You can have one big round chignon, or a small one on top of a larger one. Let your imagination be your guide. You won't need as much spray for an upsweep, but a little gentle spritz will keep the hair where it belongs.

(Right to left) Fancy upsweep, ringlets, flared ponytail

(*Right to left*) Three styles of French twist with large curls, an asymmetrical twist, and a centered roll.

What About Bangs?

I like bangs a whole lot, but I have had no success in giving my models that new (or old) and different look with bangs. Because of the way the hair is anchored inside the doll's head, bangs have a tendency to stick right straight out, and blasting them with spray doesn't help much, either.

The bangs on the Oriental Barbie® Doll stay in place pretty well because of the little plastic helmet she wears when you buy her, and because I give the bangs an occasional spritz.

I sprayed the bangs on one of these dolls straight back after brushing them to the side to see how she looks without bangs. I think Mattel should give us an Oriental Barbie® Doll without bangs, so we could have it both ways. I think that China-doll look with the regulation bangs is just a little too stereotypical, or if we must have only that look, what about cutting the hair a little shorter? I think I'd like it to be just above her shoulders, but so far I haven't quite screwed up my courage to cut it.

Another doll I wish Mattel would produce is a Carol Channing look-alike, one with the Channing hairdo, thick, puffy bangs and a sort of pageboy, porridge bowl effect. Or at least make us a really good wig. But then I suppose they would have to get into making look-alike dolls of lots of famous ladies. Maybe we should just be grateful for the variety of dolls Mattel already makes.

I have more than one hundred Barbie® Dolls now, at least six of each model, so I don't worry about changing hairdos on them for modeling purposes. I just style them and leave them, but when I didn't have so many, I found out that changing hairdos is not a problem. The spray will brush out and the hair can be washed with warm water. I have used kitchen detergent for this rather than shampoo, because the detergent is so much cheaper and it gets the job done.

Good luck with your beauty salon!

Chapter Eleven

The Props and The Photography

YOU HAVE SEEN a large variety of doll furniture and miscellaneous objects from around my house used as props in the photography of these Barbie® Doll models. I don't like the stands and I probably drove Shannon crazy (although she's too nice to say so) with my insistence on using props instead of stands. You will see lots of dolls on stands, but we used them mainly for models wearing long dresses or pants so there would be less to offend my eye.

We devised as many different ways of posing our models as we could think of, taking into account the fact that we wanted to have at least 150 pictures in addition to the cover and the centerfold shots, and feeling a constant pressure of time.

As Shannon got more and more interested and absorbed in this photography, she started buying props to augment those I had already bought, and she came up with two absolutely marvelous ideas. She bought the first wicker settee used for these pictures in a secondhand store in Salt Lake City, where she lives. I had a tiny wicker chest that I have used for many years as a jewelry box, and of the first pictures she took, that chest was used in several. We talked about the need for different textures in the pictures, something I hadn't considered at all. She showed me some of the nature scenes she had shot as a photography student, pointing out that the best of them combined very different textural elements.

I went to Salt Lake City for the first shooting. I knew Shannon was a good photographer, but after all, shooting these tiny dolls is a very special kind of photography, and while she had done some fashion photography, I wasn't secure in the thought that she could do the shooting without me there to criticize and comment. As soon as I saw the results of the first shooting, I decided to leave the models and the props with her, so thereafter she sent me the contact prints in batches of about twenty.

So let's talk about specific props now. The boxes all come from my collection of jewelry boxes. The little chests of drawers are from a variety of sources, but for the most part they were bought in secondhand stores. The little Chinese chest of drawers was given to me by a friend when she saw a few of the pictures.

After Shannon bought the first wicker settee and we had used it in some of the pictures, I was leafing through my Horchow Collection catalog one day and found they had exactly the same settee in combination with two side chairs and a small round table, the whole collection for only $12.50 brand-new. I ordered two sets to be sent directly to Shannon.

She, in the meantime, found a store in Salt Lake City that had a huge selection of miniature baskets and bought one of each, and sometimes more than one if they had both natural and unstained varieties. The flower baskets were part of that shopping trip.

The tiny ceramic vases are all secondhand. The baby grand piano, which is a music box, was bought in a San Francisco thrift shop for $3.50 with great misgivings, because I wasn't at all sure I'd be able to make it usable by painting it black. It was an ugly, flat white, with large splashy flower decals on top when I found it. I thought the scale was at least close for a prop, but I wasn't even sure of that! The black enamel used to cover it turned out all right, as you can see, but it's one of the worst painting jobs I have ever undertaken. The tiny keyboard had to be covered as I painted all around it, and when I pulled off the masking tape, I took some of the black keys with it. To paint those keys back on, I used an eyeliner brush, which worked perfectly, but of course, I dripped a tiny bit of paint on one of the white keys. I wiped it off and covered the smear with typewriter correction fluid.

The piano stool is actually a sewing cabinet for a smaller doll. After testing it for proper scale with the piano, I painted it, too. I had to rough up the varnished finish with sandpaper first, but the result is worth all the effort, I think.

Before we do another book together, Shannon and I plan to see if we can find a woodworker, hobbyist, or whatever to build us some proper Barbie ® Doll-scale furniture. If I had the time, I would take a woodworking class and learn how to do it all myself.

From top to bottom: A tiny flower basket of glazed ceramic holds porcelain roses. They are resting on a little rattan table that you have seen many times in the photos. A carved wooden jewelry box rests atop a larger, smooth wooden jewelry box. The chair to the right is manufactured by Mattel but was covered with beige glove leather before assembling. It was a bright pink color that clashed with some of the models' clothes.

This baby grand piano is a music box, which I bought in a thrift shop. It was a ghastly flat white, with flower decals, so I painted it. The stool is actually a cabinet, but since it was in perfect scale to the piano, I painted it at the same time.

Let me tell you about the sterling silver tea set. It was bought in South America about twenty years ago, and very kindly loaned to me by my friend Ann Cherekovsky, for these pictures.

Mattel makes lots of doll furniture, most of which (if not all) is plastic. It comes in some pretty garish colors, so where we used it, I covered it with glove leather in neutral colors. I don't like plastic furniture at all, for anything, least of all for high fashion photography, but one has to use what is available. I have seen lots of beautiful wooden furniture for doll houses, but it is all for smaller dolls—mostly for eight-inch dolls.

The Photography

We have already discussed some of the elements that go into photographing these little models. Now we will talk about more specific problems.

When we started shooting the pictures, I had about twenty-five dolls, so we were constantly changing clothes and hairstyles—wasting a lot of time. It was not workable or efficient, so I bought a hundred new dolls, at least six of each ethnic doll. We found that two of the blond dolls didn't photograph well so we stopped using them, but you will see a few examples of them. They are the Western Barbie® Doll and the Pretty Changes Barbie® Doll, and the reasons we didn't like to use them is that their skin tones are too pink, and they aren't the prettiest blondes, anyway. The Golden Dreams Barbie® Doll is my favorite blonde, as you can probably figure out for yourself by the number of times she is shown.

We needed a variety of hairstyles for each model, depending on the kind of ensemble she was modeling, so we spent one whole

A collection of small chests bought in various thrift shops since I started to write this book. The little Chinese chest is topped by a glass and brass jewelry box full of dried flowers. There is nothing unusual about the other two chests—standard doll furniture.

afternoon styling hair, leaving the dolls on stands with their hair held in place with clips and sprayed stiff as a board. Shannon came up with the idea of shooting them with the clips in for before and after pictures in Chapter Ten, Hairstyling. We were very tempted to cut the Scottish Barbie® Doll's hair for her upsweep because it is very long hair to begin with, but since we had only the one Scottish Barbie® Doll, we decided not to risk ruining her. I tried in vain to find more Scottish Barbie® Dolls. Shannon called every toy store in Salt Lake City and I called every one in San Francisco. It is to be hoped that we will have more of her before another book.

It never occurred to me that photographing these beautiful little models would be anything but a breeze and pure fun. After all, they can't get up and storm out if they become bored or if an insensitive photographer of-

fends their delicate sensibilities. They aren't going to behave like a temperamental live model, and theoretically at least, they will hold whatever pose they are placed in. Also, we didn't have to worry about meeting a payroll with them.

My first surprise was that they don't necessarily hold their poses, no matter how well they are positioned. They have to be very carefully posed and properly balanced.

It is actually possible to pose two or even three dolls without stands and without props to lean against, if you bend one knee of each doll very slightly, push her other leg behind as if she is in motion, and then brace the dolls against each other.

Notice that I say this is possible. It ain't easy! The slightest movement will cause such precariously balanced dolls to topple over. If one starts to go, all will go. The only reason

A whole collection of props used for our pictures. The little center table, made of rattan (I think), supports a tiny basket of strawflowers. The porcelain roses, held by a little copper pitcher (perfect scale) bought in a secondhand store, are once more shown to advantage. These roses are so tiny they would look terrible in the vase on the other side holding lilies of the valley.

This collection of wicker furniture, bought from the catalog from Horchow, a mail-order house in Dallas, Texas, is the best stuff I've found anywhere outside of the Mattel furniture manufactured just for the Barbie® Dolls. The scale is just right, though the settee is not quite long enough for two dolls to sit together. It looks like real furniture, doesn't it?

Another look at the two Mattel chairs covered with very soft glove leather to hide the neon-pink seats that clash with almost all the clothes in the collection. They are separated by a small square basket that does double duty as an end table or a lamp table.

we didn't do more shots this way is that it takes too much time, and it really takes two people, one to stand there holding her breath as she holds the dolls. She must be prepared to catch them when they start to topple, while the photographer gets behind the camera and makes sure everything is in focus before shooting. So most of our photos are taken with props or stands; either a jewelry box to brace the model against, or a chair or settee for her to sit on.

We had some hilarious moments of dolls falling straight over on their faces, even when they were sitting, if we perched them too close to the edge. In very early shots we used florist's clay to hold their feet in position, but we abandoned that later because the clay sticks to the floor even after the model is moved, and it takes too much time to wipe it off. If you look very carefully, you may find some pictures with smeary looks on the floor. It is florist's clay.

We started out using grass-cloth wallpaper for our backdrop, but switched to regular photographer backdrop rolls of paper, because we could just roll it down, and because we could easily switch colors.

A small wicker box with an interesting weave, which I use for a jewelry box, sits on the table you have seen in so many of the pictures. The basket next to the table was bought for texture contrast. The standing suitcase is made of cardboard, both sides covered with labels from all over the world.

Index

Note: Page references in *italics* are to photographs.

Accessories, 141, *160*, 161–65, *162–64*, *166*

Barbie® Doll:
   idealized figure of, 59–60
   photographing of, 183–84
   straight-arm vs. bent-arm, 143–44
   use of, as model, 13–14
Basket weave, 19
Basting, 18, 23
Bathrobe(s) (negligee; peignor), *88*, 89–93, *89*, *91–95*, *99–101*
   pattern for, 90–91
Bedjacket, *92*, 95, *95*
Belts, *68*, 141, 161, *164*
Blouse(s), *28*, *40*, *47*, *57*, 60–61, *61*, 64–65, *67*, *80*, *81*, 122
   pattern for, 65
Bra, 83, *85*, *86*
Brocade:
   attaching fur to, 150
   for coats, 143, 144
   for evening gowns, 109, 110
Brooke Shields doll, 13
Buccaneer pants, *28*, *29*, *37*, *41*, 51
   pattern for, 50

Camisole, 83, 84, *84*, *86*, *87*
   pattern for, 84

Cape, *116*, *158*, 159
   pattern for, 157
Cardigan, *37*, *39*, *40*, *48*, *52*, *76*
   pattern for, 38
Chalk, 18
Checks, 21
Christie® Doll as model, 13–14
Circle skirt evening gown, *80*, 103, *105*, 113, 121–22
   pattern for, 119
Closets for doll clothes, 11–12
Coats, *57*, *58*, *63*, *70*, *89*, *115*, 143–53, *153*
   everyday, 150–53
   long, 143–44, *146*, *147*, 149–50, *149*, *151*, *152*
   pattern (long), 148
   pattern (single-piece), 144
   single-piece, 144–49
Color coordination, 20–21, 27
Commercial dollclothes, 11, 15, 43
   lingerie, 83
Commercial patterns, 11
Crochet hooks, 18
Cutting, 18, 25
   fur, 131, 135
   leather, 73

Darts, 21, 24, 43
   in pants, 43
Dickies, 11, *66*, 161
Drapery fringe for evening dresses, *104*, 113–14, *113*

Dress(es), *57, 58,* 60–61, *61–63, 67, 77, 79*
    bodice for, 60–61, 64–65
    pajama/nightgown pattern for, 64–65
    See also Evening gowns; Tunic dress;
        Wedding dresses

Elastic waists, 43
Evening gowns, 103–29, *104–8, 111–16,*
        120–22, 124–29, 134, 155
    circle skirt, *80,* 103, *105,* 113, 121–22
    patterns for, 117–19, 123
    strapless, 103, *112,* 114–18
    toga sheath, 103, *108,* 114, *115,* 122, *122*

Fabric(s), 18–22
    categorization of, 18–19
    combination of, 20–21, 27
    cutting, 18, 25
    for evening gowns, 109
    and fit, 45
    natural vs. synthetic, 19, 20
    sources for, 19–20
    types of weaves and knits, 19
    waste, 90
    weight of, 21
Fake fur, *126,* 136, *137, 147*
Fantasy, play and, 15
Fashion vs. style, 59
Fit, 45, 60
Flounced skirts, 16–17, *47*
Fur, 131–36
    choice of type, 132
    cutting, 131, 135
    fake, *126,* 136, *137, 147*
    lining, 135
    sewing, 135
    trim, 150, *151, 152, 158*
Fur coat(s), *104, 108, 126, 127,* 132–34, 135,
        139, 140, 147, 148–50, *149*
    pattern for, 148
Fusion tape, 24, 45, 49, 93, 129

Gilmour, Shannon, 11–13, 181–86
Gloves as source of leather, 73–74, *73, 74,*
        136, 141
Gluing:
    fur, 150
    leather, 30, 49–51, 74–75, 138–41

Hairstyles, *26, 28, 40, 41, 79,* 175–79,
        177–79

photography and, 183–84
Half slip, 83, 85, *85–87*
    pattern for, 85
Harem pants, 51, *52*
    pattern for, 50
Harem top, 51
Hats, *42, 43,* 46, *58,* 68, 71, 73, *79,* 125, *137,*
        141, *164,* 165, *166*
    patterns for, 167
Hemming, 23, 24
    pattern indication for, 30
Hughes, Jennifer, 12, 13

Inverted-pleat skirts, 72–73

Jackets, *40, 46, 47, 53, 61, 64, 70, 71,* 73–75,
        77, 78, 81, 89, 100, 107, 153–55
    leather, 73–74
    pattern for, 154
    See also Bedjacket; Pajamas
Jewelry, *67, 68, 81, 111, 122,* 161
Jogging pants, 51, *51, 52*
    pattern for, 50
Jogging top, 51

Keeler, Edy, 13
Kick-pleat skirts, 72–73, *73*
Kilt skirts, 72
Knickers, *47,* 51, *53, 63*
Knits, 19

Lace, 20, 109–10
    for evening gowns, 109–10
    for trim, 93
Lamé, 109
Leather:
    for accessories, 141
    general instructions, 73–75, 136–41
    gluing, 30, 49–51, 74–75, 138–41
    for pants, 45, 49–51
    vest in, 30
Lining fur, 135

Marking, 24–25
Material, *see* Fabric(s)
Mattel Corporation, 13–14

Needle threader, 18
Negligee, *see* Bathrobe(s)
Nightgown, *89,* 100
    pattern for, 96

Non-wovens, defined, 19

Pajamas, *87, 92, 94, 97, 98, 99, 101*
    adaptation for dresses and blouses, *62,*
        64–65
    pants for, *92, 97, 97, 100*
    pattern for, 96
Pants, *25, 26, 28, 29, 37, 40–43, 43–51,*
        45–53, 58, 61, 70, 81, 132–34
    basic pattern for, 44
    finishing hems on, 45
    patterns for variations, 50
    variations, *28, 29, 37, 41, 47,* 51, *51–53, 63*
Pantsuits, *41, 42, 46, 66, 74, 79, 138*
Patterned fabric, 21
Patterns, commercial, 11
Pegboard for storage of clothes, 18
Peignor, *see* Bathrobe(s)
Photography, 183–86
Pinking shears, 18
Pipe cleaners, 141
Plaids, 21
Plain weave, defined, 19
Playing and fantasy, 15
Pleated skirt, *59,* 72–73
Printed fabric, 21
"Production-line" sewing, 17
Props, 15, 181–83, *182–87*
Purses, 141, *162*

Rawstron, Paige, 11–13
Rib weave, 19
Robe, *see* Bathrobe(s)
Role-playing, 15
Ruffled dresses, *106, 107,* 110, *120*
Ruffling, 23

Satin weave, defined, 19
Scarves, *37, 41,* 161, *163*
Scissors, 18
Seams, 23–24
    pattern indication for, 30
Setting up, 16
Sewing machines, 16, 23
Shantung, 19
Shawls, 159
    pattern for, 157
Sheath dress, *see* Toga sheath evening dress
Shirt, *see* Blouse(s)
Shirt-sweater, *25–26, 26, 28, 40–42, 45,*
        47–49, 75

pattern for, 27
Silkies, 18
Skirt(s), 61–64, *64, 71, 76, 78, 80, 137*
    flounced, 16–17, *47*
    pleated, *59,* 72–73
Sleeveboard, 18
Slip, *see* Half slip
Steamers, 21
Stoles, *107, 116, 124, 126,* 155, 159
    pattern for, 156
Storage, 11–12, 18
Strapless evening gown, 103, *112,* 114–17
    patterns for, 117, 118
Stuart, Marion, 12–13
Style vs. fashion, 59
Suede, natural, 19
Suits, *56, 57, 61,* 73–75, *73, 75, 77, 78*
    See also Jackets; Pants; Pantsuits; Skirt(s)
Sweater, *see* Shirt-sweater

Tape needle, 18
Toga sheath evening dress, 103, *108,* 114,
        115, 122, *122*
    pattern for, 123
Tools, basic, 17–18
Trim for robe, 93
Tucking, 23
Tunic dress, *66, 68, 68*
    pattern for, 69
Turtleneck, *25, 29, 37, 39, 40–42, 46, 48, 80*
    pattern for, 38
Twill weave, defined, 19

Ultrasuede, 19, 20

Vest, 30
Victoria's Secret (store), 83

Waistband:
    elastic, 43
    for pleated skirt, 72
Warp knits, defined, 19
Weaves, types of, 19
Wedding dresses, *168,* 169–71, *170–73*
Weft knits, defined, 19
Whipstitch, 27, 39
Woolf, Marion, 13

Zigzag stitching, 25, 26, 39

Hi, it's me!

Yvonne Rawstron